The wreck of the Seladon

A True Survival On An Island Story

Niulakita * Tuvalu
Stavanger * Norway

Wincent Rege
Eli Rege
Malvin Rege

Contents

Preface

On my journey to Niulakita and the islands of Tuvalu in 2008, I experienced that people became very interested in my story about the Norwegian sailors that over 100 years ago had saved their lives on their island. The idea struck me that it would be desirable to bring along a book that tells the story in English.

Since I was planning another trip to the same area, my wife and I started to write down some selected excerpts from the letters that the Seladon crew had written. These would later be translated into English. That was the start of a project that eventually ended up as this little book. We hope it can be pleasant reading for both young and old.

The original letters and most newspaper articles we have quoted from are available in the book "Seladon - An account of the shipwreck and the crew's stay on Sofia Island", which was first published in 1897 by Stavanger Aftenblad (Local Stavanger newspaper). This book was our main information source and the information from it has been used freely to tell the story chronologically and in the manner we wanted.

Sola, Norway, September 2011
Wincent Rege

The Pacific Ocean 1896

In the morning of August 8th, 1896 sails were hoisted on board two frail lifeboats that in haste had been lowered in the dark of night. A northern course was set. The ship "Seladon" that the crew had abandoned the night before was left as a wreck in the surf behind them.

With eight men in each lifeboat they put out on a voyage that they did not know where would end. On board they had only a container of water, some bread and some canned goods.

In order to save their lives, they were now dependent on either being found by a ship, or to save themselves by coming ashore on a nearby island. But the ocean was vast, and an island would be almost impossible to find. A map and a compass had they managed to save, but the navigation instruments enabling them to navigate the ocean had been left behind on the ship.

This was the beginning of a 3000 kilometer long lifeboat journey where they would face the worst of hazards and distress.

***

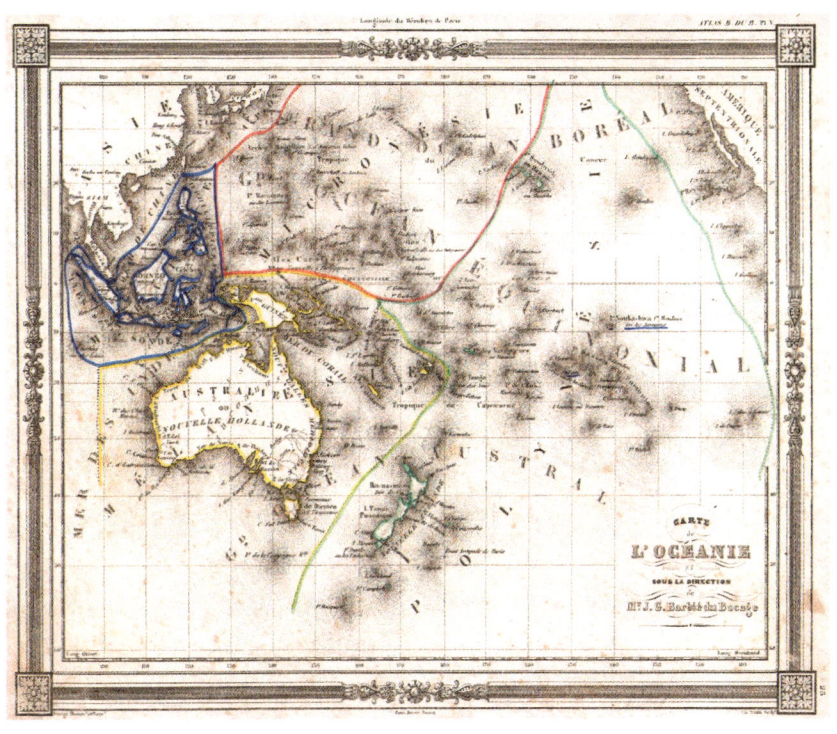

The Pacific Ocean.
Map from 1852.

The sail ship Seladon

Photo of the Seladon. The picture is taken in the English town Cowes, where the ship was repaired and re-rigged in 1891. Photo: Unknown photographer / MUST - Stavanger Maritime Museum.

The sail ship Seladon was built in the Norwegian city of Drammen in 1876 by the then widely known shipbuilder Jorgensen and Knutsen. The ship was originally built as a full-rigged ship with three masts. The cargo volume was 1066 net register-ton, making it one of the largest among the Norwegian-built sailing ships. Stavanger had at that time several hundred cargo ships on all oceans. The Seladon was one of Stavanger's most beautiful and sturdy sailing ships from this era. It had been built exceptionally sleek with fine lines, hence a really sharp sailing ship.

Drawing of the Seladon. Here rigged as a barque.
The cargo capacity of the ship was 530 commerce lest.

Commerce lest is a an old way of measure the cargo capacity on ships. In Norway, one lest was 2080-2300 kg depending on the size of the ship.

The Seladon was owned by the ship owning company Gundersen & Son together with several other business men from the city of Stavanger that had invested in the ship. At that time it was common for several people sharing the ownership of ships, these were called part-ship-owners companies. With this arrangement, the ship's earnings and risks were spread across several interests in case of loss of the ship or if there was a economic downturn in the industry.

Stavanger's proud sailing ship experienced good fortune for many years. Often the journey went to Asia with a cargo of sugar, spices, rice and exotic timber back to Europe. Many a storm had been ridden off over the years, but one day in 1891 disaster struck. The Seladon was hit by a steamship in the English Channel and had to go to England for repairs.

After the repairs, the vessels rig was changed from a full-rigged ship to a barque. That meant that the number of sails in the rig was changed and the requirement for the number of sailors on board could be reduced from 22 to 16. Many Tall Ships were at that time rigged the same way, due to the ship-owners desire to reduce costs.

In 1892, Adolph Emil Jaeger from Stavanger became the ship's new master and part owner. With a reduced crew and number of sail, it was the new master's task to make up the loss. The cost of the repairs of the ship amounted to nearly half of the Seladon's building costs in 1876.

The days of glory for these proud swans of the oceans would soon be over. With the industrial revolution well underway, the wooden ships of this type would soon be replaced by faster and safer steamships with engine power and steel hulls. The steamships used coal as fuel. Ironically the Seladon was loaded with coal when it departed on its final voyage on July 13th, 1896 from Australia.

The journey was to go across the Pacific to the new industrial superpower the United States' outer outpost, Hawaii.

Master Adolph Emil Jaeger.
Photo: Private family picture.

The shipwreck

The Seladon embarked on its final voyage from the port of Newcastle, located just north of the city of Sydney, on the east coast of Australia. The passage over the ocean was estimated to take approximately 45 days.

Two weeks had passed, Fiji was already passed, and the Seladon continued onward making good speed in an easterly direction approaching the equator. But one night the ship came too close to one of the dangerous reefs that surrounds and protects the small islands in the Pacific. In the bosom of the coral reef was the Seladon's fate sealed.

Among the crew was the 25 year old ordinary seaman Ingebret Hognestad from Stavanger. Many years later while sitting at home in his own house in Pedersgaten in Stavanger he told what happened onwards:

Ingebret Hognestad - Ordinary seamen.
Photo: Jacobsen /MUST- Stavanger Maritime Museum.

I had just been involved in the Stavanger ship Dagny's terrible shipwreck near the Irish coast where we were hit by four hurricanes in the course of one week. While sinking, we were fortunately rescued by a line ship. But I was young and adventurous, and did not become discouraged. With pleasure I signed on as an ordinary seaman on the barque Seladon that was docked in London.

From London we went to Sweden and from there in October 1895 to South Africa. After that we departed for Australia, where we arrived in May 1896. From Australia we departed on July 13th, with a cargo of coal bound for Hawaii. The weather was nice, we had a good trade-wind and all seemed well and good. But then a pitch-dark night, I was suddenly roused. We had hit one of the numerous coral islands that are to find in the Pacific. We heard the roar of enormous breakers and expected the rig to snap at any moment.

We did not have any davits[1] for the lifeboats at all, but in all haste we rigged pulleys in the yards and managed to put two lifeboats on the water. While abandoning the ship we were only able to take with us a bag of biscuits, some tins of canned food and kegs of water.

Until the break of dawn, we stayed close to the Seladon with our lifeboats. We had salvaged the maps and a compass and wanted to attempt to get an octant[2] and a chronometer[3] and some more supplies from inside the wreck. But when dawn broke we saw that it was impossible to get on board.

The surf was now a breaking distance from the ship and she was now almost a total wreck. She was now listing and most of the rig had gone overboard. We could now see the island we had run into. It was very small and uninhabited, looking quite barren. Moreover large swells were breaking making it impossible to come ashore.

---

1 Cranes for lowering lifeboats into the water.
2 Navigation instrument.
3 A navigation clock.

In a letter written by the crew a year later, the circumstances of the accident was described in this way:

... we embarked ... with accommodating wind and weather. Each day we sailed with a hope of a fast journey to Honolulu, but man predicts and God rules ... during the night of Saturday August 7th at about the hour of 23:30 with a speed of 6 knots we struck Starbuck Island. We tried to go in reverse by adjusting the rig in an attempt to get the ship free, but to no avail. A quarter of an hour later we sounded the pumps and found four feet of water in the room. We then started to put two of the largest lifeboats on the water, supplied each of them with a small keg of water, a ¼ sack of bread, canned goods, meat, salmon and sardines.

When the ship was rocking obsessively and the rig was about to fall down and perhaps injure both people and lifeboats we decided to enter the lifeboats and abandon the ship to its own fate. We abandoned the vessel approximately at 01.00 hours and rowed some distance away from the ship and rested on the oars and waited for the break of dawn to see if we had the opportunity to get on board and rescue some navigation instruments and an almanac that was left behind when we went in the lifeboats.

But when daylight came, we saw that the ship had worked its way further into the surf and the waves were breaking over the amidships, making it impossible to get on board. The site where we ran aground was a small guano island with a height of 5 meters above sea level, uninhabited and without a place for getting ashore. So there was nothing else for us to do but to steer for the nearest inhabited place, since we had maps and a compass in each lifeboat.

The name of the island that the Seladon had run aground on was Starbuck Island, an uninhabited coral island located at 5 ° 28' South, 155 ° 52' West in the Pacific. It was 9 km long and 3.5 km at it's widest. There was very little vegetation on the island, only a few palm trees and no water. Because of dual coral reefs off the shore and its low height of only five meters above sea level, the island was one of the Pacific's many ship graveyards. Since it was discovered by Valentine Starbuck aboard the whaling ship "L'Aigle" in 1823, has it been a snare for at least three known ships. March 10th, 1870, ran the French transport ship "Euryale" aground and sank. The captain and his crew of 35 people managed to get ashore on the island and lived there for over a month before being rescued by a passing ship.

The crew of the Seladon never got ashore on Starbuck Island, but formerly used names of this inhospitable island may indicate that survival there over a longer time would probably not have been possible. Other names of the island were in fact Barren Island, Hero Island and finally the ominous Starve Island ... !

The desolate landscape of Starbuck Island.
Photo: Angela K.Kepler/Wikipedia Commons/CC-BY-2.0.

Starbuck Island circled on the map.

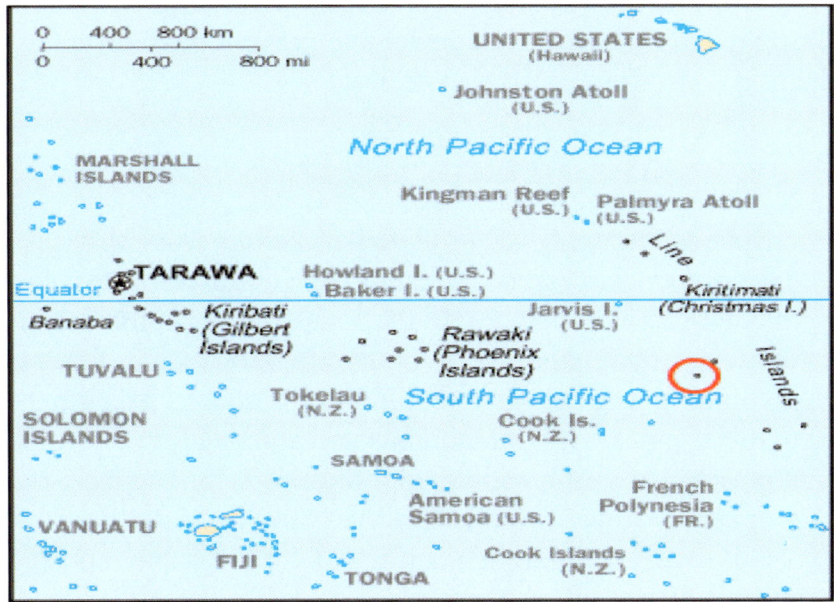

The lifeboat journey

The lifeboats journey the first week:

The crew now set sail for the nearest known island called Malden Island. It was only 200 kilometers away in a north-easterly direction. This was a distance they had the hope to cover in a couple of days. They assumed that there were people on the island since the excavation of huge deposits of guano[1] took place there at the time.

The lifeboats, which the crew called "Storbaten" (the large boat) and "The jib", were rigged for sailing with eight men in each boat. Both boats were in a rickety condition and had to be bailed constantly since they were very leaky. "Storbåten" could hold a speed up to 6 knots, while the "jig" was slower, had a tendency to drift off course and was almost falling apart. The men on board lashed it with ropes in the best way they could. Soon a rope was drawn between the boats, in order to hold contact and prevent them form drifting apart from each other at night.

---

1 Guano is a term for accumulated droppings from birds and bats. Guano can be added to poor farming soil to make it more productive. In the 1800s, this resource was a very important commodity. In dry climates such as that of the Pacific islands, where colonies of birds had been able to breed protected from humans and animals for thousands of years, could meter high deposits of guano be recovered. Towards the end of the 1800s and into the 1900s, every atoll in the Pacific was explored and tapped for this important resource.

The crew described the lifeboat journey from the site of the shipwreck and towards the Malden Island[1] in the letter that they wrote:

When we left the ship behind, we set sails on both lifeboats and headed for Malden Island in a northerly direction. The same day we started with small rations of food and water. We started with two meals a day, one at six in the morning and one at six in the evening. The ration consisted of four tablespoons of water for every man, some bread and a half of a salmon-roe for breakfast, the other half for supper.

The steward of the crew, the 35-year-old Lars Marthinius Tonnesen from Stavanger, described the start of the lifeboat journey in one of his many personal letters that he wrote in his diary. These words were written before he knew how it would end. The letters were addressed to his wife and two children at home in Norway:

We had to disregard what was to be our fate and headed out on the endless, wide ocean. We had no navigation instruments, just a map that the captain brought along. But what was out there, far from people? ... We had to find out.

We had saved a little food; we had a keg of water in each boat and 50 pounds of bread. Oh no, it wasn't much. Oh my dearly beloved, it was not much to live on. Just imagine how we had to ration from the first moment. We headed for the closest Island ...

---

1 Malden Island is today uninhabited. It rises only 10 meters above sea level and is known for its prehistoric ruins and the numbers of seabirds that nest there.

Steward Lars Marthinius Tonnesen.
Photo: Jacobsen /MUST- Stavanger Maritime Museum.

August 9th, after sailing north for two days they expected to
have reached the level of Malden Island. When nightfall
came, they turned about and tacked to the south-east with a
small sail and low speed to avoid getting too far north while
it was dark. At first light, they sailed north again all the
while longingly looking for the island. To their despair, they
saw nothing but blue ocean as far as the eye could see.
Tonnesen continues:

... but to our great sorrow, we did not find it. Then all
seemed hopeless for us. We cried and prayed day and night
for ourselves and our loved ones at home. And our prayers
were heard, our strength was not crushed. It was hard to
see our hope fade, but with renewed strength, we
continued on. May God help us.

They continued now onward further north to the next island marked on the map; Christmas Island. It had its name from the famous British explorer Captain James Cook that discovered the island on Christmas Eve in 1777. The island was 700 km away in a north-westerly direction.

... that same evening we decided to head for Christmas Island, which was about 6 degrees further north, we would have to cross the equator ... The captain's illness intensified now for each day, because he was as wet as the rest of us as there was nothing we could do about it, since we had entered the lifeboats in just what we were wearing at the time and thought that it would just be a matter of rowing ashore onto the island we had run into. We did not think that this would become a month's voyage with food and water that would have been suitable for a two day pleasure trip for 16 men.

This week started the sufferings, the hunger and the thirst. In particular, the thirst was the worst. Being so near to the equator, there was no shade from the sun. Too hot by day and too cold at night. Soaked most of the time. Being wet at day was ok, because when the shirt dried we took it off and dipped it in water and put it back on again, wet. It helped for the thirst, but at night we froze.
(From the crew's letter)

...The days passed but to no avail. The worst was when after being in the boats for eight days, we almost ran out of water, although we had used it with the utmost care. We handed out to each man two small wine glasses morning and evening. During the day it was awful to bear, at night it was better when it came to the thirst, but on the other hand we froze to the point as not to endure, soaked to the skin as we were, by the spray. (From Tonnesen's letter)

The lifeboats journey the second week:

After a week in the lifeboats, they were running out of water. The situation was critical. Rations had been reduced to a spoonful of water in the morning and evening, when it fortunately started to rain on the eighth day. That it started to rain just when they needed it the most, was a stroke of luck, since the area around Christmas Island is considered a equatorial desert zone where there on regular basis are long dry periods without any precipitation.

We changed watch every four hours and during which we all prayed for rain. And thank God, we didn't wait long before it finally came. At last we got to drink our fill. Being thirsty is the worst there is! (From Tonnesen's letter)

... Saturday August 15th, we were able to fill up our water supply in both lifeboats which was a great joy for us. The bread had been spoiled at once as it had become wet the first night, but it tasted good anyway.

Sunday the 16th, we assumed that we had sailed the distance between Malden Island and Christmas Island. Now we were again disappointed in the hope of seeing land. We had a man in the masthead, morning, noon and night as long as he had the strength to climb up. Christmas Island was supposed to be about 150 km in circumference but about even with the sea level.

Now, we talked with them in the second boat on what we should do. The captain said there was nothing to be done, we could only entrust ourselves to fate. Perhaps we would meet a naval vessel, a steamer or a sailing ship. In the evening we turned southwest. On Monday we continued on a south-westerly course and we held this course to possibly reach Samoa or Fiji. (From the crew's letter)

After a nine-day voyage toward a possible rescue on the islands to the north, the course was changed to the west. Here the ship traffic was greater, and there were islands that they might reach while still alive. The weather had so far been fairly good, but this would not last.

The boats were old and leaky, so we had to bail constantly, otherwise those who slept in the bottom of the boats on their off duty period would drown. We got wet of course, but the sun came up by day and dried us. Wet and dry, dry and wet, it was not easy to endure. Every day we expected that we would find a new island, but every day in vain.

Tuesday August 18th, we sailed directly under the weather with the other boat in tow. At four o'clock in the afternoon we had an accident with the boat we towed. It was capsized by a large swell with the sad consequence that our dear first mate drowned. We almost lost our carpenter as well. Fortunately, we finally got a hold of him, but we all had to put our life on the line to rescue him. The boat heeled in a horrid rough sea, and we were attempting at the same time to rescue our shipmates. Now, we were 15 men in our boat with only the upper board over the water.
(From Tonnesen's letter)

More details about their friend's drowning were given in an interview that Stavanger Aftenblad had with the crew at a later time. The 25-year-old mate Kristian Nielsen from Stavanger had been lying on the long seat aft on the jigg[1] and tried to get some sleep. He sank without being seen or heard of when the boat capsized and they saw him no more.

Three of the others managed to get up on the keel of the capsized boat, while three pulled themselves over to the large boat with the help of the tow line between the boats.

---

1   A jigg is a type of boat with a deck aft, which ends in a straight sill. Because of this construction, a man can lie across the seat all the way aft in the boat.

The carpenter Tollak Olsen Vestbo struggled in the water for a long time, until one of the men in the boat stretched out a leg that he got a hold of. He was then helped on board. They also managed to recover the keg of water from the capsized boat.

The waves that night ran high and with fifteen men in one boat there was almost no freeboard that separated them from the water. The capsized boat was still hanging by the tow line and served as a drift anchor and assisted them through the storm. That evening nothing was eaten, just the usual water ration was dealt. During the night the wind fortunately subsided a bit.

The next day they were able to turn the capsized boat right side up and found with joy a tin of meat, a can of sardines and a can of salmon under the keel. The boat was as expected damaged and unusable. They left it behind.

The end of the second week of the voyage is described in the crew's letter:

The suffering increased now for each day. Our facial skin became burnt and fell off, the lips were cracked by the lack of water and around the waist and hips we got great sores from lying in the boat and from filing of our wet clothes against our skin while rowing. This week, we had several showers and rain, so we had to take down the sail and let the boat drift with the weather and wind in a north-westerly direction.

The lifeboat journey the third week

Now the hunger increased. We only got a couple of bits of bread, but no one complained. All were in agreement to stretch the rations as far as possible, on the chance we were lucky enough to reach an island. The worst thing was that when we were thinking of food, it seemed like it was melting in our mouths. (From Tonnesen's letter)

The Master Adolph Emil Jaeger had a wife and three children at home in Stavanger. Jaeger was only 43 years old, but was ill and had used medication daily even before the Seladon left Australia. The crew believed that he suffered from tuberculosis since he was coughing so much, both before and after the ships accident. During the lifeboat voyage he became weaker and weaker each day.

On the morning of Sunday of August 23, the last ration of bread was handed out, but it no longer looked like bread. The captain's illness still increased. The carpenter became ill also and lost a lot of weight, something we all did, but this was too much for an old man, he was in his sixties.

Monday the 24th of August, another day of mourning. At 5 PM the captain died quiet and calm. We sewed him into a sack and at seven o'clock, we handed him over in prayer and singing of hymns to the great, mysterious sea. The hymn "Hvo veed hvor nar mig er min ende" (Who Knows how near is my end) we sang with tears on our cheeks while our dear captain's body quickly sank into his seaweed covered grave. (From the crew's letter)

The crew had now been in the lifeboats for 17 days. With two men already dead, they continued to sail in a south-westerly direction, hoping for a miracle in the form of an island or a ship.

The Seladon's mizensail was cut into small square pieces and we made a knot in each corner. Now these canvas pieces served as hats and protected our heads against the equator's burning sun. Now we also had to reduce the rations of canned food, sometimes just one meal a day, but water still twice a day.

We continued sailing in the hope to reach land very soon. We had six men on each watch, three men to steer and three men taking turns bailing the boat because it was very leaky ... some flying-fish that landed in the boat was eaten at once and also all the long-necks[1] that attached themselves to the boat was eaten and they tasted good. The last ten-ration box was divided into 56 parts; it would last for four days. Monday morning August 31st, we took the last ration of meat and still no land in sight.

Lars M. Tonnesen wrote about the only thing they saw when they looked for other boats or islands:

In the 30 days we were at sea in the lifeboats, there were no signs of any other life other than a lot of sharks that followed the boat and occasionally biting the boat and the rudder so we thought it would break straight off. We tried to catch them, but we failed. But it is certain that had we caught one, we would have devoured it raw with the greatest of appetite.

---

1 Long-necks- Crustaceans that stuck to the boat below the waterline.

The life boat journey the fourth week

After 23 days was the food at an end. The sun was right above them and sent its merciless and stinging rays down over the crew. Without food and with the strict rationing of the water, they suffered terribly. Their tongues were swollen, their lips were full of sores and they were weak and discouraged. Most had given up all hope of a rescue.

We sailed day after day without seeing anything. We cried ourselves to sleep and when our off duty period came, numerous and heartfelt prayers were directed to heaven. May we reach land. LAND! LAND! It looked dark from our point of view. September 1st, the food simply ran out, but we were still alive, but our life-force was diminishing and we were quite faint.

Tuesday, Wednesday, Thursday, one day after another came, wore off under hunger, thirst, loss and exertion. Still nothing to see, just the infinite ocean. We were the only ones alive as far as the eye could see.

Then, on Sunday afternoon of September 7th, just as I took over the rudder, I caught sight of an island. Land, land it sounded inside me, but I could not say anything in the first seconds. I turned the rudder over and headed for the small black dot in the distance.

We have land boys, I finally got out. You can believe that there was joy. Some cheered. Others cried of joy.
(From Tonnesen's letter)

The crew was too weak to row, but with the help of the sails they approached the island quickly. The spark of life returned suddenly to the crew which the last six days had been exhausted and without food.

Soon they could see that it was a lush little island, densely covered with coconut palms.

The rescue was near, but the danger was not over. Around the whole island there was a dangerous reef. When the deep and free Pacific Ocean rolls its heavy waves upon shallower waters and hits the coral reef, the forces of nature is released in an inferno of chaos where people and small boats can do little.

The men sailed for a while along the oval island to find an opening in the reef, but found none. The ocean current pulled the boat closer and closer to shore, and the roar from the breakers became increasingly stronger. With full sails and two men at each oar, they steered without the fear of death straight toward the white crest of foaming breakers.

... there were heavy breakers along the shore, so we dared not to attempt to land. Then we saw to our delight, some people on the beach. It began to get dark, but they lit a large bonfire that we steered toward. Closer and closer we came, and soon we were right in the middle of the surf. It thundered and foamed around us. After a few minutes' struggle, a big breaker capsized the boat. Most clung to the boat, but I and a few others jumped into the water in the hope that the current and perhaps the breakers would bring us to shore. I struggled fiercely, of all my strength, and thanks to God I got ashore. Exhausted, bruised and almost unconscious. I was rescued. All 14 were rescued.

The people received us with the utmost of kindness, and brought us home to their houses where they gave us food and drink. And then, my dearly beloved wife, you can believe that the food tasted, even though we were so exhausted that we could hardly move our hand to our mouth. Who could expect otherwise after that we for six days and nights had not seen food and after the hard struggle with the breakers. (From Tonnesen's letter)

After 30 days in the lifeboat, the men could finally feel dry land under their feet. Up the steep beach the survivors, staggered, crawled and limped towards the natives huts. The landing was hard, the lifeboat was completely smashed. The sail maker Peder Thime had received a serious injury to his foot as they struggled with the boat on the reef, but they had all survived. The natives of the island had been fearful when they saw an unknown boat coming towards them. The men had armed themselves with knives and the women had run off to the woods, but as soon as they understood that the Norwegians were peaceful seamen they helped and cared for them as best they could.

10 ½ months as islanders

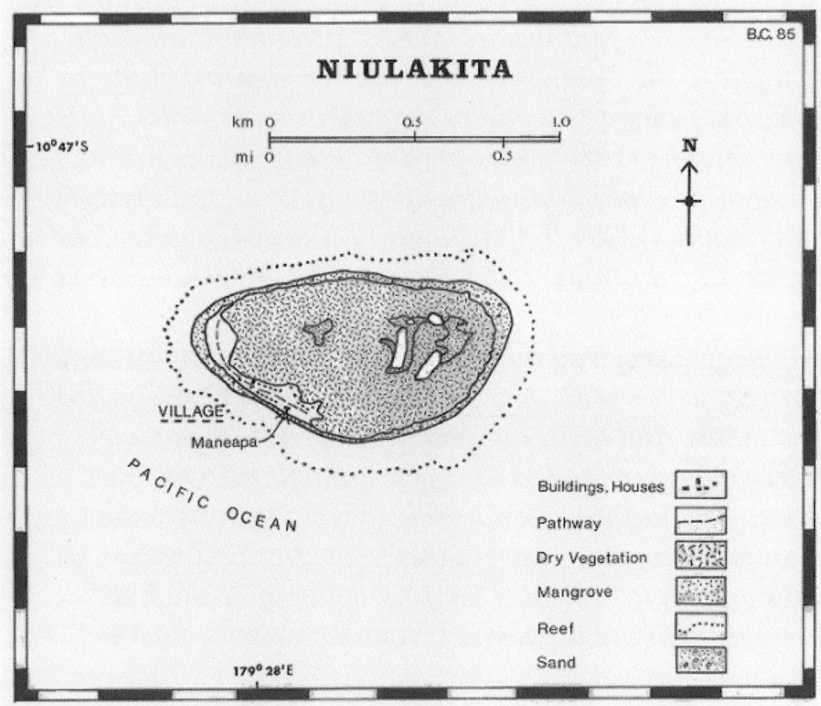

The island Niulakita that the men had landed on was the
island that seafarers called Sophia Island. The coral island
was only a kilometre long and half a kilometer wide. The
island was lush with tall coconut palms and in the middle of
the island there were several small ponds. There lived two
families, a total of ten people on the island when the
Norwegians arrived.

For a whole week the men were nursed by the island's residents in their house before they slowly regained their health, but for the oldest among them, the 56 year old carpenter Tollak Olsen Vestbo from Sandeid, the strain had been too much. He was mostly unconscious and did not eat anything at all. Only occasionally did his friends have contact with him. When he began to talk in a daze, they decided to keep watch over him day and night, one person on each shift.

On the night of Monday September 14th, he died quietly and peacefully. The next morning they started to make a coffin and arrange a burial place. At noon the same day they held a funeral service with prayers and hymns both at the house and by the grave. His name, the day of his death and his hometown were carved into a large rock that was placed at the grave.

The carpenter would not properly recover. He had received a sad break during the voyage. Nothing helped, his days were numbered. After just an eight day stay on the island, we had to walk the heavy steps to his grave. The dead man's coffin was adorned with leaves, so pretty it was.
(From Tonnesen's letter)

For the newly arrived sailors, the days on the island soon fell into a regular routine. The days were used to obtain substantial food and drink to survive. The sources of food that existed on the small island had to be utilized to the fullest.

A month after we arrived on the island, as our health returned, we started to provide our own food. We went around on the island and kept an eye out for the turtles when they came to lay their eggs. That happened at night at high tide. During the day, some men went into the woods and brought home firewood. Others brought home coconuts. Some cleared away trees and planted bananas. So we were at work at all times ... Healthy, temperate climate and comfortable conditions on this island whose size is much like Solyst or Lindoy.[1] We could walk around it in 25 minutes. (From the crew's letter)

Bird Hunting

The island was abundant in seabirds. They were black and looked like crows. First, we started taking all the eggs, then we took all the young and then when they came to an end, we started on the adults. But it was hard work. It was best when it was windy and rained. Once it was dark, two and two went out on bird hunting without any clothes on,

---

1 Islands around Stavanger.

34

just a piece of silk around the waist or a "lava lava" as the islanders called it. If there was moonlight, we had to wait until it was completely dark; it had to be completely dark. We had to climb trees and catch them with our bare hands as they slept ... we stretched our hand out as far as we could reach, grabbed the bird with a quick grip around the legs, twisted their neck and stuffed them under the belt we had around our waist. 15 to 20 birds could be caught in this way and brought home. But there was not much meat on them, once they were plucked. You needed six to seven of them for a man to get a decent meal. The women prepared the bird meal for us. The birds tasted good, but had a trace of fish oil taste. (From the crew's letter)

"The island was abundant in seabirds; they were black and looked like crows."
Black Noddy, a seabird of the tern family.

Ingebret Hognestad had his own original method to kill the birds. He explained:

It was important to seize the birds with one hand and hold on with the other. Then I quickly bit over their throat in order not to scare off the other birds!

Turtle Hunting

... It came slowly and majestically, breathing heavily, up the beach. It sounded like a whale or a porpoise when she stopped to catch her breath. Then she again took hold with her huge paws and waddled up the beach until she found the spot in the sand she searched.

We had to be careful when it was to be captured. If she was allowed to hit with her paws, she could kill a man. Two men had to get both their hands under the side of her shell. So with a firm grip rolled them over on their back. Then they could bring them to the ponds on the east side of the island. The eggs were a delicacy. They were the size of egg yolks, and a turtle could contain 500 - 600 eggs.

The meat tasted like beef and could be prepared as steaks or meatballs. This kept on until Christmas, then the turtles stopped coming ashore. This turtle catching could not be resumed until July the following year. From the turtle shell, several of us made jewellery, necklaces and watch chains. For tools we used knives, nails and steel wire.
(From the crew's letter)

Photo: Algy O`Comnel.
Wikipedia Commons/Public Domain.

The Banana

The Banana was an unknown fruit in Norway 100 years ago, but through the newspaper "Stavanger Aftenblad" the crew could subsequently tell about this nutritious fruit that had helped them stay alive on the island:

The Banana is a long fruit from a tree with the shape of a plump carrot. Green when unripe and yellow when ripe. With a thick skin that must be peeled off. When it is boiled unripe, it has a taste much like the potato. Ripe it is sweet and very tasty. By putting it down into a sandy hollow in the ground, and by placing branches and leaves over it, you can have it ripe in a few days. It thrived on the island, and they could plant as many Banana palms as they wanted. (From the crew's letter)

Fishing in the ponds and in the sea

Besides turtles, birds and bananas to eat, they caught eels in one of the ponds in the centre of the island. They used a steel wire hook that they had made, and with it they were sometimes able to yank the occasional eel. The women on the island were better anglers, they swam under water with a net between their hands and with a lightning quick motion, they managed to catch the eel in the net. A little fishing in the sea was also attempted. Some small sharks were caught, but their taste was not pleasing. Closer to land there was a lot of beautiful small fish that the Norwegians found fascinating:

Along the shore there were many small fish of a wide variety and with marvelous shapes and colors. Some looked like half moons. The eyes could be in the front, side, under, across and so on to infinity ... there was very little taste from them compared to the eel that tasted excellent. (From the crew's letter)

The Coconut Palms

The Coconut Palm was exploited in several ways. They
could drink the sweet and savoury liquid from unripe nuts.
In the ripe fruit the color of the liquid turned white and had a
stronger taste. But they could also tap the sap from the tree
where the coconuts started to develop. By making an
incision up in the palm tree, they released a white liquid that
resembled wine, which they called Calevy. Three or four
bottles of this drink could be gathered daily by hanging
bottles in the tree where the liquid steadily dripped from the
incision. The Norwegians thought this drink was very tasty,
and it became their favourite drink while on the island.

Many of the crew were skilled craftsmen and used the shells
from both coconuts and turtles to make jewellery and
ornaments. A number of ornaments that they made are still
in Stavanger, privately owned by the descendents of the
crew.

The residents of the island

When the Norwegians arrived, there were a total of ten people on the island. It was Dick[1] (26 years) with his wife and four children, and his brother Belly (40 years) with his wife, they had no children. In addition, there were two servant girls.

The inhabitants had lived and cared for the island for eight years on behalf of the island's owner, the American Harry Jay Moors. Their work consisted of removing the grass and vegetation in order to plant banana palms. They also worked to produce copra.[2] The natives spoke a little English, so it was possible for them to communicate with the shipwrecked men. English they had learned from 60 workers who had recently been on the island to excavate guano. The workers had left the island a few months before the Norwegians arrived. The crew described the natives and the their way of life like this:

... they are from Rotuma and belongs to the people Nates. They have a dark complexion and are Christian people. Their nose is a little flat and they have dark brown eyes. Two of the women had black curly hair.

Rainwater was collected from the roof to the tanks below; there was no well water to be found anywhere. Every four months or so, the owner of the island sends provisions, beans, rice and salt ship biscuits. On workdays they wore

---

1 Dick was nicknamed Dill.
2 Copra is the dried meat from the coconut. It is used for the production of margarine, coconut oil and soap and is still an export commodity from many islands in the Pacific.

only a sack around their waist but on Sundays they were fully dressed. When there was a party for the family, a birthday or alike, they always roasted a whole pig. They roasted the whole pig on a stone, and had a very solemn and happy time together. They prayed and sang and praised God in their own way. (From the crew's letter)

On October 16 there was a very sad incident on the island. Dick, one of the native brothers, got a splinter of bone in his foot while walking along the beach. The foot became infected and he contracted blood poisoning. Two people watched over him in shifts while he was ill. Just before he died, while in the arms of cabin boy Thomas Berentsen, he asked his brother to take care of his wife and children. On the night of Sunday October 25, he died and was buried in the same manner as Tollak Olsen.

The cultural differences between the Norwegian sailors and the natives could at times create conflicts between them, since they lived so closely together on the small island. The religious Norwegians were among other things, not very impressed by the devotion of their brothers in the faith. This was expressed in this way:

Otherwise were these people's Christianity so - so ... immediately after the Sunday worship they could resume their usual life with bad language, cursing and swearing ... on Sunday though, although they did not do their customary every day work, they lived in the same manner as all other days. (From the crew's letter)

After some time, Belly, the surviving brother, took one of the servant girls as his co-wife. Their wedding tradition was such that they roasted a pig, then ate and exchanged the chewed food with each other. Afterwards the party continued with dancing and music. The Norwegians did not like this marriage at all, polygamy was an unheard practice for them and also the girl was very young. They also felt sorry for Belly's first wife who had to participate in the celebration of the marriage. The marriage may have been triggered by some sort of jealousy towards the Norwegians.

The new life as islanders was not always pleasant and comfortable:

There were an endless number of rats. They swarmed all over, in the fields and in the houses. They were the size of a large mouse. Some very intimate objects. As we slept at night, they would come and start picking between your toes, and yes, around your mouth also. When we got tired of their crawling, we seized them with our hands and threw them against the wall. Sometimes the floor was covered by dead rats. One of the guys was pretty angry when he woke up one morning and discovered that there was a thick layer of rats under him. He thought someone had done it as a prank. But no, it just happened by chance.

... Otherwise it was a comfortable and carefree life, without a thought about what the next day would bring. Our greatest grief was the thought that our loved ones mourned us as dead.

The steward Lars M. Tonnesen described in a letter, the loss and longing he had for them at home:

I want to write to you to let you know that the good God has saved me from a watery grave and brought me happy and safe to this island, where we now live and every day await a steamboat that will take us away from here.

... We have been here for three weeks now. They have been long weeks and God only knows how long we will have to stay here. Every day my longing to see you becomes more painful and greater. I think of you that soon expect that we arrive in Honolulu and will soon learn that nothing is heard from us. Then the grief takes you too my dear. But a higher power has the control, he will change this from grief to joy. The joy of hearing that we are alive. I wonder if help is coming soon.

Oh, yes! Now it is not long before Christmas is here, then certainly God will make it so that I can come home to you. Oh, I feel I can see my small ones, how big they have grown. Little Margit and little Trygve. All I have to do during the day, is to go around on the island and collect shells for Margit, and believe me, here is a lot of them.

My dearest wife and children. Three months have now passed since I started to write these words. Every day I have waited for a chance to leave here, but it looks like it is going to take time. I am still with good health, but my dearest, the longing and grief is killing me. We must, must get help soon! Eight months have now passed since they saw a steam ship here.

There is only 10 days until Christmas, but where's the joy? Just sorrow. Only sorrow. You have sorrow. I have sorrow. No Christmas joy you have, long ago dressed in mourning I see you, may God help us, it is my hope and my prayer.

On June 25th, 1897 Tonnesen continues his last letter he wrote on the island:

Now I have been here on the island nearly a year. Every day I have waited for a chance to leave this place.

My dear ones, I have mourned and waited for so long now. Sometimes I get the idea that I will never see you again, but a mightier one rules. Sorrow can soon turn into joy. It is difficult to stay here, but we are grateful for our food and drink, there was a time we did not even had that.

You have probably given up hope now, that I am alive, but I hope that I will see you all again. The star that smiles at me, will also shine for you.

My dear, I am writing this in case something should happen to me. I hope then that these words will reach you.

The Norwegians scouted at all times after a ship that could bring them back to civilization. The natives had told them that soon a boat would come with supplies.

The supply boat had been there four months earlier, before the sailors arrived and would soon return again, the natives reassured them. But the weeks and months went by without any boat arriving. In fact, they never saw anything of this boat in the 10 months they were there.

But now and then they saw ships far away that they attempted to contact, and one day in mid-July they finally succeeded:

On October 30th, 1896 we saw a sail in the horizon, but to no avail because the breakers were too big so we could not launch the boat.

On Friday the 18th, of June 1897, we saw a steamer come into view. We went to the boat and came happy and well through the surf, but again to no avail.

On Saturday the 17th, of July, we saw again something on the horizon. We went in the boat, and when it turned to come close to the island to check if something was wrong there, we quickly approached the ship.

When the ships crew learned that we had been stranded 10 months and 11 days here, they took our boat in tow and went close to the island and took the rest of us aboard.
(From the crew's letter)

The ship that the Norwegians had managed to get in contact with was the steamer "Clyde", which was a surveillance ship from Fiji. It had gone close to Niulakita because the captain wanted to check his position and his navigation instruments.

The ship was to visit Funafuti and Rotuma before returning to Fiji. There was not really enough food on board the "Clyde" to accommodate the 13 sailors. At first, they would not take them with them and suggested instead to retrieve them later, but the Norwegians did not agree to this. Finally, it came to that they took four live turtles on board as their own provisions. These they had captured on the island and were taken from the one pond where they at the most had 20 turtles fenced in.

About the parting with the natives, Ingebret Hognestad told later: *It was not to be denied that the natives of the island were sad when we left them. We had lived so long together and shared both good and bad. We, on our side looked forward to coming home, although we had many good memories from the island.*

The phrase about the «sad natives» was probably an understatement. Both the islanders and the leaving men must have reflected on the fact that they would never meet again. Some of the involved may very well have been more sad than others … and that is as far as we in this book will go on speculating on possible romantic relations between the two worlds.

Nevertheless one can easily imagine that especially the women and children were heartbroken when the gentle and exotic sailors suddenly was gone. The names and later destiny of the unsung female heroes that took care of the stranded men remains unknown.

The journey on board the "Clyde" took 16 days. On August 2nd, 1897 they arrived in Suva harbour, the capital of Fiji. Incidentally, in Fiji the Norwegian barque "Ellen" was ready for departure. The barque home port was the town Grimstad, and had a Norwegian master and crew. It was now arranged that the 13 could follow the ship on to Australia via New Zealand. After a few days, while new clothing was found for the new crew, they went on with the Norwegian sailing ship. The passage to Sydney was estimated to take approximately a month.

On board the "Clyde" there had been a doctor named B. G. Corney. A few days after arriving in Fiji, he sent a letter to the British consul in Oslo. In his letter he told of the shipwrecked Norwegians that they had picked up and taken with them:

To her British Majesty's Consulate General in Christiania Suva, Fiji August 5th, 1897.

I have the honour to tell, that I under an official trip to Funafuti and Rotuma in the district of Fiji by the steamer "Clyde", in July got the island Niurakita, which on some maps is known as Sophia Island, in sight, as the captain wanted to verify the longitude and control his chronometer.

As we approached the island on July 17th, five men met us in a boat that they had launched from the beach to attract our attention. They told us that they and eight others staying on the island, were the survivors of the crew of the barque Seladon of Stavanger, and that their ship had stranded on Starbuck Island during the night of 7th and 8th August 1896 while they were sailing from Newcastle, Australia to Honolulu with coal.

The second mate Olaus Lode said that Captain Adolph Jaeger died in the boat 16 days after they had left the wreck, the mate Kristian Nielsen drowned when another boat capsized in a squall at night to August 18th, and that the carpenter Tollag Olsen died on Niurakita 9 days after they had come ashore, as a result of long starvation and suffering.

... I consider it my duty to take this opportunity to as soon as possible make you aware of these circumstances and as a notification to the Norwegian government, so that the crew's relatives and the Seladon's company can receive this notification, without delay, since so much time has passed, since the bark is likely to be listed as missing, and especially when I understand that some of the survivors, as well as the dead captain were married people.

... When they reached Niurakita they had been 6 days complete devoid of nourishment, and for 3 days before that they had only a simple can of meat to share. The lifeboat journey lasted for 30 days. I need not say that it has been of great satisfaction for Captain Callaghan and I to have been able to contribute to these poor people's rescue, after being trapped for 10 ½ months on the Niurakita.

We were not able to make it especially comfortable for them; the "Clyde" is a small steam yacht of 61 tons and was not equipped for an event like this. The men brought, however, 4 turtles with them when we took them aboard, and we cared for them as well as we could. In total they were with us for 16 day, where 5 days were spent on land on Rotuma and 2 days on Funafuti. Their conduct was always exemplary.

B. Glanville Corney, Chief physician of Fiji.

Sign of life from the crew

Back in Norway, people had long ago given up hope of finding the crew alive. The ship Seladon was supposed to have arrived in Hawaii almost a year ago. The shipping company sent in December 1896 a worried telegram to Hawaii where it was asked for any sign of life from the missing Norwegians. In January 1897 a discouraging reply was received. Stavanger Aftenblad wrote:

Received reply today that the Seladon was neither seen nor heard from. The time needed to sail from Newcastle to Honolulu is 45 to 50 days. Now it's been 180 days, so it must have gone down ...

But then the newspaper added something interesting:

It is not impossible that the crew may have come ashore on one of the thousands of islands in the ocean and may still be living there.

The families mourned these 16 men, that they thought was lost forever, and some had announced their loved one's death in the newspapers. One was so sure they were dead, that the shipping company had already paid out life insurance to the bereaved. But then, late on Saturday night of August 21, 1897 there was a knock on the door to Lars Oftedal, the founder and editor of Stavanger Aftenblad. It was a messenger standing outside with a telegram from New Zealand.

When Lars began to read it, he was very surprised:

21-8-97, London Reuter.
Auckland, New Zealand.

Today, they arrived here the survivors from the Stavanger barque Seladon that for over a year ago left Newcastle for Honolulu. The Seladon was wrecked in August at the Starbuck Island. After great hardships and longing, the crew reached Sophia Island and remained there for 10 months living with friendly natives. The captain, the carpenter and a sailor are dead. A steamer came to their rescue and brought them here.

Lars Oftedal later described in his newspaper how he was shocked of the unexpected telegram:

Our astonishment and joy can better be thought than described with words. Our first thought fell on the first officer on board, since his grieving parents lived across the street, and since his girlfriend and sister were our acquaintances ... We therefore rushed over and told the dear parents the good news. Such glad tidings can cause a great strain. Even strong people can get heart problems just from joy. Therefore, we used great care. Oh, what joy there was!

Oftedal immediately brought the news to the ship owners and to others who he believed had not gone to bed yet. Messengers were sent out to the crew's families with the happy news. Already at 23:00 hours were copies of the sensational telegram posted in Miss Sylvia Krags shop window in Kirkegaten 2, and in the windows of the Aftenbladet's reception in Soregata 26. Soon many people stood in front of the windows reading the posted news about the Seladon crew. Into the wee hours, people were standing and discussing the sensational news. A father read of his dear son, who he was sure was dead, but now was found alive. In joy he personally thanked the newspaper's secretary with a handshake for this great posting.

The next day, which was a Sunday, another six postings were put up around the city. Within a few hours, the incredible news spread throughout the district, and was of course everyone's topic of conversation. Handshakes and congratulations were exchanged. Maps were studied, and people speculated how it all had happened. Crew lists was reviewed, three men were dead, but the names of the survivors was not yet confirmed. People waited with expectation for new newspaper reports that could provide more information about these 13 men who almost had risen from the dead.

Kirkegaten in the 1890s. Sylvia Krags shop in Kirkegaten 2 is the small house that juts slightly out into the street. Photo: Dreyer Publishers A/S.

Stavanger Aftenblad brings the news that the survivors of the Seladon are found. Monday August 23rd 1897.

Lars Oftedal, the founder of Stavanger Aftenblad.
Photo: Stavanger Aftenblad.

The crew list

Master Adolph Emil Jaeger
Stavanger, 43 years old, married
Born July 1, 1853

1. Mate Kristian Nielsen
Stavanger, 25 years old, unmarried

2. Mate Olaus Olsen Lode
Stavanger, 39 years old, married
Born October 1, 1853

Steward Lars Marthinius Tonnesen
Stavanger, 35 years old, married
Born January 14, 1862

Sail maker Peder Thime
Stavanger, 31 years old, unmarried
Born July 7, 1866

Sailor Marcelius Aske
Stavanger, 36 years old, married
Born October 10, 1860

Sailor Gabriel Johnsen
Stavanger, 30 years old, married
Born July 24, 1867

Sailor Carl Ingvald Thorsen (Stolsvik)
Stavanger, 24 years old, unmarried
Born September 20, 1872

Sailor Abraham Hallvardson Tjelta
Stavanger, 22 years old, unmarried
Born January 8, 1875

Sailor Hans Johan Jensen
Karmoy, 25 years old, unmarried
Born September 20, 1872

Deckhand Andreas Jakobsen
Stavanger, 23 years old, unmarried
Born November 11, 1873

Deckhand Ingebret Hognestad.
Stavanger, 26 years old, unmarried
Born June 6, 1871

Jung Sailor John Kristian Knudsen
Bergen, 19 years old, unmarried
Born October 10, 1877

Jung Sailor Hans Tollefsen
Stavanger, 19 years old, unmarried
Born January 10, 1878

Carpenter Tollak Olsen Vestbo
Sandeid, 56 years old, married
Born November 28, 1839

Cabin boy Thomas Berentsen
Stavanger, 20 years old, unmarried
Born July 14, 1877

Soregata 26 where Stavanger Aftenblad was started in 1893.
The telegram that told about the survivors
of the Seladon was posted in the window.
Drawing: Henry Imsland from a book by Ingvar Molaugs
w/others: The last words are never said, 1968.

Soregata 26 in Stavanger. Picture taken in 2011.

Lars Oftedal was a well known man in Stavanger. Through his newspaper, he would now be the one who described the mood of the city. Oftedal was a versatile man. He had previously worked as a teacher, sailor priest, preacher and a parish priest. He represented the Liberal Party in Parliament for two periods and sat on the city council for a total of 14 years. In Stavanger, he ran social work among the city's population and ran for a time his own "care services group" and built schools, factories and orphanages. He was also a newspaper man and founded the newspaper Vestlandsposten in 1878.

Over the years he had published many religious pamphlets and books. After he resigned as a priest, he founded the newspaper Stavanger Aftenblad in 1893.

Oftedal was a skilled editor who wrote and edited his newspaper in a down to earth manner. He had a personal and distinctive style that became very popular among the mainstream of the population. His newspaper soon became the largest in the district. Although Oftedal was a controversial priest and politician, his opponents had to be impressed by his enormous work capacity and his care for the poor in the city.

The first telegram that Oftedal received, had said that one sailor was perished. The uncertainty was therefore great for the families of all the five sailors. They did not know which of them had died.

In a telegram from Stavanger to New Zealand it was asked for the names of the deceased. August 23rd came an answer that only made the uncertainty even greater:

Special Telegram August 23rd 1897 to Stavanger Aftenblad through NTB Auckland, New Zealand:

The 3 dead of the crew of the Seladon are:

Capt. Adolf Jaeger
Carpenter Tollak Olsen
Sailor Christian Nelsian

In the telegram it said again that one sailor was among the dead, and that his name was Christian Nelsian. But the problem was that there was no sailor in the crew with this name.

In doubt the newspaper editors chose to assume that the name Nelsian was a misspelling of the name Knutsen. Thus, the newspapers reported that the sailor who died was the 20-year-old Johannes Kristian Knutsen from Bergen. After several telegrams back and forth it was finally discovered that the dead man was the 25 year-old first mate Kristian Nielsen, who had drowned when the lifeboat capsized.

Lars Oftedal was a close neighbour of the family of the dead officer. It was to them he had rushed over with the glad tidings that night when the telegram came. Once again the hope burst for the mate's family and fiancé that for a few days had looked forward to seeing their Kristian again.

The misunderstanding was due to the English word "mate" that had been incorrectly translated into matros (sailor) in the telegram. Oftedal was in despair over the mistake that had been made:

There we sat in sorrow and pain. Due to an erroneous translation's fault. In all this pain there is a bright spot: Both are not dead ... Knudsen's family, who after yesterday' newspapers had to believe that their relative was gone, have today a happy day ...

He immediately wrote a personal letter to the mother of Johannes Kristian Knudsen and told her that her son was among the survivors. The mother later sent a thank you letter back. The letter shows how important religion was to people along the west coast around this time.

It was hard times for the mothers at that time in many ways. They often had many children and struggled hard. Both husbands and sons worked often as sailors. Over 60 000 Norwegian men worked on cargo ships in the late 1800's.

The Norwegian sailing ships was a dangerous place of work and casualties were high. A total of 182 Norwegian ships were lost only in the year 1896, which amounted to 6 percent of the Norwegian fleet.

Should the worst happen that the breadwinner died at sea, the poor-relief fund was not far off for the family. At such times it helped to have a strong faith. It could give peace for the yearning and the fear that the women had for their men at sea and provide comfort when the tragedy struck.

The letter that the mother of Kristian Johannes Knutsen wrote to Lars Oftedal read:

A heartfelt thanks for what you wrote! It was for me more than dear to read about your involvement in my son Johannes' rescue. My joy as a mother was indescribable, when I after many days of longing learned that he lives, and I really dare hope to see him again in this life.

I have the firm hope that the Lord that always listens to the cries of his children now has won his heart, and that will delight me the most. There can still be new dangers that threaten my young boy, but may He who has so miraculously saved him, also now be with him on his journey home.

And when the last journey has ended, lead him to the eternal peaceful residents where no danger threatens and where changes are no more. Only then will my joy be complete. With heartfelt thanks for your kindness, I send you my warmest greetings.

Hoglandsdalen September 3, 1897 Kristine Ovreeide.

The Return journey

Meanwhile on the other side of the globe the crew continued on their long journey back to Stavanger. On board the barque "Ellen" they finally got to taste Norwegian food again and they were able to tell about their experiences to other Norwegian seamen. But it is not to be denied that the men had been sceptical and anxious when they once again had to go aboard a sailing ship to get from Fiji to Australia. One of them said later that when the ship heeled in the storm, he stood on deck shaking like a willow leaf. The strains were still hard for the body, and the nerves were frayed after all that they had been through.

The crew arrived in Sydney on August 28th. The 19 year old sailor Thomas Berentsen wrote about the wonderful welcome they received there, in a letter he wrote home. In Sydney the Norwegians got a preview of what awaited them at home in Stavanger where Lars Oftedal and others were busy planning the return of Stavanger's now famous boys.

We had no sooner come ashore before we were taken to the "Sailors Home". There came consul Falstad in the evening and visited us and orientated us that the continuation of our journey home would start in nine days. You can believe how happy we were when we learned that we were going home by steamer, for we dreaded going aboard a sailing ship again. Clothing was to be provided on Monday, so the first Sunday we had to stay inside. We had received trousers, shirts and boots on Fiji. They were so big that there was room for two of us in them. On Sunday we were visited by several Norwegians. Including a number of people from Stavanger. They were keen to find out how we were. On Thursday we were invited to a French dinner with John Grannes. He was from Stavanger, and owned one of the largest hotels here. We were about 30 people in all, only Scandinavian, including the Norwegian- Swedish consul. We sat at the table for three to four hours, where speeches were held for us and for old Norway. After the meal, refreshments and cigars were served. We entertained the guests by singing Norwegian songs we had sung on the island during our long stay there. Between one and two o'clock at night we went our separate ways from a very pleasant evening that we would always remember.

Saturday night was a highlight for us. Then consul Falstad invited us to a theatre prepared just for us. As we came in, we got such loud and long applause from the audience that it was impossible to hear ourselves speak. The hall was beautifully decorated with Swedish and Norwegian flags. A large Norwegian flag was placed right in front of us up on the stage. It was an entertaining evening, in fact it was mostly young ladies that danced and sang so it was a pleasure to watch.

On Monday September 6th, the crew went aboard the large steamer "Orizaba" and left Sydney with a light heart. This ship would bring them to London with an expected arrival in one and a half months.

The voyage home took them down the coast of Australia, visiting Melbourne, Port Adelaide and Albany before crossing the Indian Ocean to Sri Lanka. From there through the Suez Canal and out into the Mediterranean Sea. They rounded Gibraltar and followed a course directly north toward England. On October 21st, 1897 the ship arrived in London.

In London, no representatives of the Norwegian authorities showed up to greet them and to help them on to Norway. Neither the Norwegian consul nor the Seamen's priest for London was to be seen.

Editor Lars Oftedal that had always stood up for the disadvantaged among the population criticized strongly the lack of a reception of the shipwrecked sailors. He believed that this was disrespectful conduct, and that this clearly showed the class distinction in society that he fought against:

Every stevedore and stoker on the London docks knew about the Seladon's crew and their amazing rescue, they had read about it in the newspapers. These people also knew the exact time of the arrival, they had also read that in the papers.

The consul in London knew nothing. He was just as ignorant as the wise men in Jerusalem about such things. At least he pretended not to know. And when they came to London, there was no one to meet them. Not even the seamen's priest, who however, arrived the next day to accompany the crew to the consular office and later arranged a ride for some of them in the city, was present at the steam ship's arrival. Nor his assistant.

They therefore had set off on their own to the train station and waited there like deserted sheep late at night, for so to take the train up to the "Sailors home", where the landlady treated them to food. When they arrived at the consul's office the next day, the priest and the first officer went into the office and organized the trip to Newcastle. The others waited outside. The consul did not even see them.

That's the way it is, when someone is great and fine and exalted above ordinary humanity. Most often no interests in what is small and abandoned in life. No interests other than what is related to themselves and their large food supply ...

It seems to us quite likely that he could have shown a little interest to greet these so amazingly rescued sailors and at least could have shaken their hand. No. "It is none of my business." An evening meal for them or at least a meeting with them in the church had been quite natural. No, none of these.

Newcastle was the last stop on the long journey home before the trip across the North Sea. That the Norwegian consul in Newcastle sent a staff member to follow the crew on board the ship to Stavanger did not satisfy Oftedal who continued his class struggle and compared the efforts of the Norwegian representatives in England in the following way:

... Just like when someone here sends a man down to "Ryfylkekaien" (the docks) to collect a herd of sheep coming by boat to town. No one to greet them neither in London nor Newcastle.

***

The homecoming

In October 1897 it was two months since the telegram telling of the survivors from the Seladon, had been announced. In Stavanger, people were now waiting for the crew to come home. Lars Oftedal kept the interest alive with his daily articles about the case in his newspaper.

The steamship "Venus" had been in regular service between Bergen-Newcastle-Stavanger since 1893. Now people started showing up at the dock whenever the ship arrived in Stavanger to see if it had the sailors from the Seladon on board. But every time, the city residents had to return home disappointed.

Skoltegrunnskaien (dock) in Bergen 1925.

Closest is the coastal steamer DS "Kong Haakon".Just behind is the Bergenske Damskipselskabs DS "Venus" which was the "England boat" that went between Bergen-Stavanger-England. The ship to the left is unknown, and in the background is the DS"Stavangerfjord" from the Norwegian America Line. Photo: Anders Beer Wilse/Norwegian museum of culturalhistory/Wikipedia Commons.

Finally there came a message from England that the crew had gone aboard the DS "Venus" and was on their way home. Here we'll let Lars Oftedal tell us what happened in Stavanger, a cold October night in 1897:

... Then a telegram came: "Departure Venus on Saturday 23rd, October." Saturday passed, and Sunday slipped slowly away. All longed for the moment when Venus' lanterns could be seen. It was worst for those who had their son, their brother or their father on board. For them, the day was endless. They had no peace of soul and mind. They tidied up at home to make everything right for a pleasant welcome, and then they had to make a trip to the dock to look for the ship, although it was hours before it was to be there.

By nine o'clock Sunday night, the streets were filled with people, young and old. Seladon, Seladon buzzed in ones ears. A telephone message was to come from Kvitsøy when DS Venus passed by, but no message came...The minutes passed. "Oh, no, now it is too dark for the ship to dock. And this fog. There will be no Venus before tomorrow." These were the words of all the seamen. And the fog didn't lift, it just got thicker and thicker, but the people did not give up. It was cock full of people on the pier. And they all saw lanterns on the fjord. "There it is! Look there! That is for sure a lantern!" But the customs officers shook their heads, because that type of lanterns was always on the fjord.

The clock went to 00.00 - 00.30 - 01.00 and the occasional person crept home; it was as if they were ashamed to go. Most people persevered. Turned the coat collars up to keep the night chill and the fog out, stamped their feet, moved around and stared and stared. They felt that they just had to greet the Seladon boys already this evening. There were policemen among the crowd, but they had a quiet night, for a quieter crowd could not be found anywhere, no shouting, no mayhem!

It was predominantly whole families that were out. The old weather-beaten sea dog staggered back and forth with their wives, they had to see to their proud successors of the seas. And Stavanger's young people, yes they had to greet those who now stood before them as their greatest heroes and role models.

The clock in the tower struck 1:30, and it was like there were hours in between when it sounded two strokes. Then they heard a long hoarse howl from far out on the fjord. The crowd livened up. They listened. Another howl. The excitement rose. Numerous that had gone to bed, got their clothes back on. There were thousands at the dock. They clung to the sides of the warehouses. Each herring barrel gave space for two to three people. All stared out toward the fjord. There was the howl again, louder than the previous. There are the lanterns!

Everyone became quiet, very quiet. We stood as riveted to one spot. There they were, the thirteen boys who we thought were dead and gone. Brothers we had mourned and sons that we had wept over. No one can describe this solemn moment as the ship slipped inwards. No one said anything because no one could interpret the thoughts being born. Closer and closer the ship slipped toward the dock. Suddenly sounded the joyous tones of "Ja vi elsker" (Yes we love ... Norways national anthem) from the local brass bands into the night air. It was the first greetings to Norway's strapping seamen and instinctively thousands joined in the song, verse by verse.

The excitement and emotion had to find release. And the cheers that followed the song when "Long live Seladon's crew" was shouted was, yes, full of rejoice. Happy tears were shed and joy that never sounded more sincere. Young and old, women and children they all took part. They all used the voice they had. No one kept quiet. It was a wonderful atmosphere.

"Watch your selves!" "Venus" came alongside the dock. "Verdens Gang's"(newspaper) correspondent had the pleasure to be the first to jump aboard, even before the ship was properly moored. They rushed towards me. We exchanged greetings as if we were old acquaintances and hundreds of questions were put forward ... Never can such a moment be forgotten. Unforgettable was also the appearance of their eyes and their voice as they whispered, first one, then another, yes all of them: "Is my father and mother alive?", "Do you know if my girlfriend is alive?"

Welcome, Welcome! "There they are!" And aboard they rushed. Brothers met. A father found his son. The scenes now witnessed when they saw their loved ones, as they embraced those who were closest to their hearts, cannot be described. It is the most moving imaginable. "Is that you?" "Are you alive?"

Reverent the spectators remained standing around the family groups receiving their loved ones. These were not the scenes where you tend to have witnesses present. But who cared to think about that here? The atmosphere and the cheers seized us all. And the weather-beaten sea dogs, even their eyes glistened. "But Mom?" Yes, mother stood on the pier. And was the meeting between father and son very moving, then there is no words to describe the moment when a mother gets her son back ....

... It was nearly three in the morning when the Seladon crew walked over the gangway. When sailors normally come home, they haul heavy, big chests and sacks of clothes. And has a horse on the pier to transport their baggage. But these poor souls had no need for horses, a simple little bundle under their arm was all they had, but never has a happier crew crossed a gangway. And never has a gang of sailors received a more heartfelt and intense reception.

On the dock in Stavanger more cheers met them, and the music started to play again. The cheers rose above all limits, because we had the Seladon's crew among us. Even after it all was over, the streets were still crowded. No one could really get themselves to go home. Sure, the thirteen went. And their families. Now, it was time to rest. Now, they needed to talk together alone in peace. But in those homes, there was joy that night.

Three days after their return, there was arranged a big celebration in Stavanger's old "Salem", a chapel in Bergelandsgaten 24. Salem was one of Stavanger's largest halls, and could accommodate 3000 people. Lars Oftedal had built the hall in 1893, but sold it in 1896. Here the returned crew was to be celebrated and be welcomed home. It was the "Young Seamen's Association" that organized the event. The profits from the celebration would be given as financial assistance to the sailors, since they for such a long time had been without income.

The thirteen sailors arrived at the celebration at eight o'clock in the evening and were again greeted by applause and cheers from all the guests, as they were ushered up to their places on the podium.

The hall was packed to the full since several thousand people had met up to have a part in this event. Many were obliged to follow it all from the outside of the building. As the crew entered the hall there was much unrest and dangerous crowding when people pressed forward to catch a glimpse of the returned sailors. As the evening progressed, speeches were given by ministers, politicians and ship-owners. "Ynglinge-foreningen" (similar to YMCA) provided the musical entertainment. Stavanger Aftenblad wrote about the celebration the next day:

The celebration was extraordinarily successful. An atmosphere unlike any at a party in Stavanger.

Old Salem in Bergelandsgaten 24 where a large celebration for the returned Seladon crew was held.
Picture taken in 2011.
Today the Baptist Church uses the building.

Vagen in Stavanger. A steamer at the "Skansekai" dock.
The same place that DS "Venus"
arrived with the survivors from the Seladon.
Photo: Georg T. Monsen, 1898, Stavanger City Archive.

The DS Venus was in the route Bergen-Stavanger-Newcastle
in the period from 1893 to 1930. It was dismantled in
Stavanger in 1933.

A picture of the crew

The survivors were photographed shortly after they came home to Stavanger.

First row from the left:
Hans Tollefsen, Tomas Berentsen.

Second row from the left:
Peder Thime, Marcelius Aske, Olaus Lode, Lars Tonnesen, Gabriel Johnsen.

Third row from the left:
Johannes Knutsen, Carl Thorsen, Hans Jensen, Abraham Tjelta, Andreas Jakobsen, Ingebret Hognestad.

Photo: Jacobsen /MUST- Stavanger Maritime Museum.

Afterwards

Gradually, the festivities ended and everyday life began again for the brave sailors. It was time to move on. Work had to be found and families supported. Some were finished with the uncertain life at sea and got a job on land. Others again took berth aboard commercial ships and continued sailing on the seven seas. A couple of them sought their fortune in America and settled there.[1]

Lars Oftedal continued to publish his popular newspaper. Through articles in his newspaper he persistently argued that the Parliament should grant financial support in the form of 18 months of wages to the shipwrecked sailors, for the time that they had been without income. But he did not succeed.

Oftedal had after a while written so much about the crew's experiences that he collected the newspaper articles in a small book. The book sold in a large number and got a place on the shelf in many homes. It was later re-published in 1935 and most recently in 1997 in connection with that Stavanger was a port of call for The Tall Ships Races. Thus has his book largely contributed to that the story has become quite well known among people today, more than 100 years after the events took place. Lars Oftedal died in 1900, 61 year old. His son, also named Lars, took over as editor and ran the newspaper after his father's death.

---

1 Sailor Carl Ingvald Thorsen (Stolsvik) we know for sure later moved to Port Washington.

Captain Jaeger's tragic fate did not frighten his two sons from pursuing the same career as their father. Both his sons, Adolph and Otto became sailors and later on captains on Norwegian ships. Captain Jaeger and his wife Elizabeth Olsdatter Grannes had also a daughter, Kathinka who became the mother of a son.

„Seladon."

Forlis. Rædsomme dage. I baadene. Ti maaneder blandt vilde. Hjemover.

Pris 10 øre.
(Eftertryk forbydes.)

Sandnæs 1897.
Ingvald Dahles bogtrykkeri.

Lars Oftedal's book.

Tollak Olsen Vestbo who died on Niulakita had a wife and son at home in Sandeid. Tollak had sailed as a carpenter the last 22 years on international voyages. He had experience as a boat builder.

Shortly before the Seladon's accident, the family had lost their youngest son Konrad, by drowning. He was only 12 years old. Together with a friend they had been out in a boat on the Sandeid fjord nearby the "Opsalholmen" (small island). The boat capsized and only his friend survived. Tollak's wife, named Alette lost both one son and her husband at sea within a short time period.

Their second son, Bernhard, who was born in 1881, later became a sailor like his father. He married Malla Opsal from Vikedal and they had three children, Borghild, Amanda and Olaf. Malla died young, and Bernhard remarried with Serina Osterlid. They had four children, Toralf, Konrad, Bernhard, Ragnhild and Tora.

Tollak Olsen Vestbo.
died on Niulakita September 14th, 1896.

Alette Vestbo, the wife of Tollak lost both her husband and her son Konrad at sea.

Sandeid in Ryfylke photographed in 1956. Tollak Olsen Vestbo built the house placed nearby the water about in the middle of the picture. Below: Tollak's son, Bernhard took over his childhood home and is photographed with his 3 oldest children, his wife Serina and a neighbor girl to the right.

Lars Marthinius Tønnesen finally got home and was reunited with his wife Inger Elisabeth and the children Margit and Trygve. It was Lars that from the lifeboat discovered Niulakita as a dot far away on the horizon, and thus saved them all. His last letter was written on Fiji on the way home:

I am sure you are happy when I tell you that I am alive and well, and I hope that you are well there at home also. Yes, He has saved me. So often I have seen death before my eyes, from hunger and thirst; I have been so exhausted that I have not been able to stand on my legs. Oh, I cannot with a pen write all that I have suffered on this trip, but now I am almost with you, now I can soon join you and dear children in my arms ...

... Our stay in the boats was 30 days, 6 days quite without food. On the island we lived for 10 months and 10 day. On board the "Clyde" we were 16 days; the people here have been very kind to us and given us food and clothes. I hope you have seen something in the newspapers about us before you get this letter. If you wish, quote the most important and get it into the newspaper, Aftenbladet or give them the complete letter and let them use what they want.

Lars and Inger Elisabeth had later five children more; Tonnes, Inger, Kristiane, Ella and Leonard.

All seven children got married and had children and the descendants became numerous. Lars lived out the rest of his life as a farmer on a small farm on Kalhammeren in Stavanger.

We thank Lars for the company.

Lars M. Tonnesen. *Inger Elisabeth Tonnesen.*

Elise og Trygve Tonnesen. *Tonnes Tonnesen.*
Trygve was born 1895. *Tonnes was born 1901.*

*Kalhammeren in Stavanger. Lars M. Tonnesen's small
farm and his son Trygve's house both circled.
Photo: Dreyer Publishing A/S, year unknown.*

The Seladon's song

Again, has a half-forgotten shipwreck
veiled for forty years
taken form in a daily newspaper.
Despite that time passes,
despite that wonders happens every day,
despite the old must give way when new ones are born
there is to be found in every city a dream-sarcophagus
where the contemporary and the past meet!
Every city has its wonders that will never be forgotten,
"Seladon's shipwreck, Stavanger has its!

I see it, our city, in the semi-dark light,
the streets narrow and the houses small,
ships with husbands and lovers on them
sailing all over the world.
I sense the first icy shudder as the days passed
and nothing more was heard,
the sleepless nights, the anxious prayers,
the hope that burst and the veiled eyes
for those who were dead, husbands and sons.
I see the sails torn in the storm' thunder,
the ship disappear in the watery crater.
But look! a boat in which they shoulder to shoulder fight
against death, ship-mates! On foaming wave crests.
It dawns, it subsides, a tropical sun flames up.

A Day Has Gone
The next, yes a hundred, who feels the agony,
the courage, the forces fighting for life
against the thirst and hunger and sleep's avalanche?
The spirit of survival, - yes, but there is more:
the thought of home, not provided for loved ones,
and flaming prayers that leads to the heart's
unimaginable forces in the death struggle's pain.

I see them in veils, see the land that rises,
for dead tired eyes as elysian kingdoms,
the waving palms, the sun warmed sand
a vision of heaven when it dies in our mind!
I hear them slurp the refreshing drop
and eat and sleep slowly to life,
and wake up and hear the whisper in the reeds
in the heart the first strengthening hope.

A year has passed. It is autumn in Stavanger,
the lights are lit a Saturday evening.
In the newspaper sits a man and rests,
the bell rings. A telegram.
He opens it, reads and doubts,
"Seladon", "Seladon", can it be true?
That the ship went down but the men not?

They flew round town from house to house,
one cheered and screamed with laughter and tears.
And future castles
in rubble over the missing loved one's coffins,
was raised again in a single night!
Wonders among wonders! They are alive, they are alive!
God bless the three that death has taken,
but life took revenge on what death demanded!

I sit and read the newspaper and think:
that even in times as crazy as these, the heart breaks the
cold links by reading of the "Seledon's" shipwrecked.
It happens each day that someone is lost,
it is told every day in all the world's newspapers.
But this with the "Seladon", it is bigger,
it is more than loss, more than the word.
It is that life and faith can win over the ocean storms and
distress in ones minds.
It is the temple of manhood and courage,
for prayers, - yes , for Stavanger's blood!
It's risen from the earth for forty years to a myth in the air,
which never perishes!

Gunnar Salvesen (Poem from about 1935)

Expedition Seladon 2008
(As told by Wincent Rege)

In 2008 my cousin Ragnar Hellesto and I made an attempt to get to the island Niulakita to experience the place where the crew from the Seleadon had saved their lives. We had both grown up with the story about the Seladon's shipwreck.

One of the survivors of the shipwreck was the sailor Abraham Hallvardson Tjelta. When Abraham came home he decided to quit as a seaman. He became a farmer with a farm on Tjelta in Sola, near Stavanger. Abraham married Ane Elisabet Svensdotter and they had seven children, five boys and two girls.

The farm that he ran is close by our own farm and one of his sons, Gunnar was a good friend of ours. Abraham was regularly for years invited to speak about his experiences. One time in the 1930s, he gave a lecture on the Seladon shipwreck at the youth centre "Dasen" in Tjelta. My grandmother and my aunt were among those who attended this lecture. My aunt, who was only ten years old at the time, said she remembered how exciting it was when Abraham told about the hunt for the black birds on the island. The youth centre "Dasen" is now demolished, but the foundations still exist on our farm property.

Abraham Hallvardson Tjelta.

The Stavanger Maritime Museum arranged from January 9th to December 1st, 1998 an exhibition about the Seladon, where they among other things, displayed the jewellery that the crew had made on Niulakita.

In April of that same year, Gjert Meling, who had visited the island, held a photo lecture entitled "In the wake of the Seladon." My father Magnus Rege, my wife Eli and I were among the audience. We became highly thrilled about what we saw and heard. My father said to me: You should take along Ragnar (my cousin who was a mate on the training ship "Gann") and try to reach Niulakita. Dad had the same thought when he visited Fiji on a trip around the world in 1987.

A trip to the island in the Pacific, where Abraham and the rest of the crew found their rescue, had thus been in the back of my mind as a desire for many years, but to get there with limited funds seemed for a long time as impossible.

When I myself travelled around the world in 2007, Ragnar asked me to try to find out how we could get to Niulakita. To gather information I went to the Tuvalien Embassy in Suva in Fiji.

The residents of these small islands of Tuvalu, must necessarily from time to time receive supplies by boat, but the timing of these departures is highly uncertain. Both bad weather and other circumstances make it impossible to have stable routes. Shall one have the chance to go with such a boat, one must either have a good dose of luck or be prepared to take up residence on the main island for quite a while. The Seladon island Niulakita that we wanted to go to, is also the smallest and most inaccessible of Tuvalu's nine islands.

In January 2008, with the help of the internet and email correspondence with the Naval Department in Tuvalu, I got a hold of an itinerary showing the scheduled departure dates for the supply vessels on Tuvalu. This was perhaps the only opportunity we would get to fulfill an old dream. Should we take the chance?

On February 15th, 2008 we were on a flight from Fiji to the main island of Tuvalu called Funafuti. On my itinerary that I had brought along was the date February 19th listed as a scheduled departure of the ship "MV Nivaga II" to the island Niulakita. The return ticket we had to get back to Fiji was six weeks later. Would we succeed?

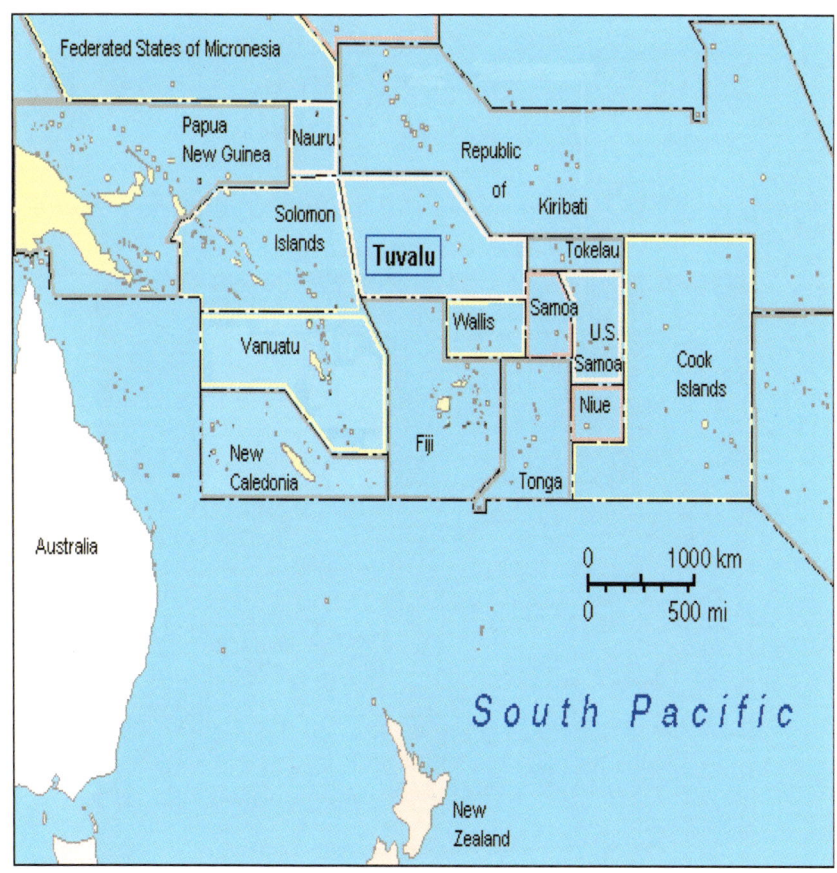

The main island Funafuti.

A picture of the village where the town hall and the airport are on Funafuti.

Shortly after we had landed, we were told that the journey would not go as planned. The disappointment of this disheartening message was of course great. The boat trip to the island had simply been cancelled because of bad weather and mechanical problems with the ship. The difficulties continued when we got to the bank on the island to take out local currency. The bank had closed for the weekend, and no ATM was to be found outside the building. As we stood there and looked somewhat longingly in through the bank windows, we saw that there was someone moving about in there. Some smiling, friendly bank employees immediately opened the door for us. I had read in the Lonely Planet travel guide that debit cards could be used on the island. For this reason we had not brought with us Tuvaluan currency. Our despair was great when the female functionaries at the bank said they had recently stopped accepting the bank cards Visa and MasterCard. We suddenly had the desire to return to Fiji with the same aircraft ...

A few notes of Australian dollars we carried we were able to exchange so that we had enough money for food and a room for a few nights. Fortunately, there was an internet connection on the island, and the bank employees helped us with information about how to transfer funds from Norway via Australia to Funafuti. Although it could take a few weeks before the money arrived, all should go well. We immediately sent the following e-mail to several family members at home in Norway and asked them to transfer money to us:

Friday February 15th, 2008: PENNILESS! The VISA machine does not work on Funafuti. Need quick supply of Australian dollars. Send 2000 Australian dollars to each of us. The first one that opens this e-mail, call the others on the phone. The procedure that the bank outlined is here ...

Soon fortune really smiled on us. Someone we chatted with told us that a delegation from the government lead by the Prime Minister Apisai Ielemia was going on an official visit to Niulakita. Would it be possible to come along with these gentlemen on their trip? We were encouraged to visit the Marine Affairs department and speak with Captain Iefata Paeniu. He had his office in the town hall.

We were very anxious when we knocked on the door. How would he greet two penniless Norwegians that wanted to travel with the Prime Minister to Niulakita? Fortunately, he was a nice man and an occupational brother of my travelling companion. We were promised that we could come along. He regretted that there was no free space on 1st class, but we accepted immediately a cabin on 2nd class. Since the trip was not to start before two weeks, the captain asked us what we had planned to do in the mean time. We shrugged our shoulders at this question. He continued: "While you are waiting, why not come along on the ship on a trip to the three northernmost islands on Monday? You can have accommodation on 1st class." We just had to admit that we only had our useless bank cards to pay with. To that he replied: "Well then I'll put up the money for you until yours comes." We gladly accepted the offer and had a brilliant five-day trip to the three islands in the north; Nanumea, Nanumaga, and Niutao.

It was exciting to experience how people lived on these tiny Pacific islands and how their small boats had to be manoeuvred to overcome obstacles such as the surf and coral reefs. Even though there now is blasted passages through the reefs, can critical situations quickly arise. On this trip we became better prepared for the upcoming trip to Niulakita that has the most difficult landing conditions. The people on board encouraged us to use a life jacket and said that we had to pack our photographic equipment in a waterproof box that would float in case the boat capsized.

On the way back to the ship after a visit to the island Nanumaga, we were witness to a dangerous situation that arose with one boat. The passengers had just boarded the boat on the beach, and were returning to the ship when the outboard motor suddenly stopped. Without engine power to keep the boat under control, it immediately turned across the waves and was about to capsize. The crew jumped routinely into the water and forced the bow of the boat up against the waves again. At the same time the boatman feverishly tried to start the engine. An attentive passenger suddenly saw that the ignition key had fallen out. Fortunately it was attached to a string. The problem was solved, and the motor was started again. The experience was so frightening that some people declined to go ashore on the island of Niutao the next day.

During the waiting time the last week before going to Niulakita, the two of us took lodgings in separate private guest houses. We also visited each our own congregation on the main island. By using these days wisely, gave us the opportunity to get to know more people and form a larger network. The first evening we ended up in a big family party in the Manuapa, which is the name of the community houses in Tuvalu. There we got our first impression of the traditional Tuvalish culture, song and dance. Another day we joined in playing volleyball in a private garden. It was also pleasant to be invited home to dinner in friendly Tuvaluan homes.

Ragnar was invited one night to participate in exciting night-fishing for flying fish in the lagoon. It was done by luring the fish with a light and capturing it with a net as it flew through the air.

We met just two tourists on Tuvalu. One of them was a retired English journalist named Rita. She spent her holidays only on Pacific islands, and had been on vacation on Tuvalu earlier. Just before we embarked on the trip to the northernmost islands, she gave me some banknotes in that she said: "In case there is some misunderstanding about the tickets, you can have this money to pay for them."

The other tourist was an American visiting the island in order to buy postage stamps. The production and sale of postage stamps as collector's items is a source of income for the country. Otherwise we met several journalists and film crews from several countries, concerned with climate changes and the effects it has on the islands. Tuvalu is often mentioned these days in connection with the fear of the sea level rise since the islands here rise just a few meters above sea level.

"MV Manufolau". The ship we followed when we visited the islands of Tuvalu.

A person that I had a conversation with gave me an idea to what the goal of my next expedition in 2012 could be. He was from the Pacific island Rotuma and was on Tuvalu to negotiate trade agreements. When we got talking about our mission to the islands, he mentioned that on the island of Rotuma there probably lived descendants of the families that lived on Niulakita at the same time as the crew from the Seladon.

We know in fact from the letters that the crew wrote that the natives at that time came from Rotuma. According to documents I came across at the university library on Fiji in 2007 there were only 4 people registered as residents on Niulakita in a census from 1911 and in 1914 the island was sold. It could mean that several of those that helped the Norwegians sailors in 1896 later moved to other islands and perhaps there told the story to their descendants. The place they most likely had moved to was the island of Rotuma.

At last the big day had arrived, the departure to Niulakita. We met up at the ship "MV Manufolau" in due time. The ship's crew had dressed up in white for the occasion, and stood solemnly lined up to receive the Prime Minister and his party on the dock. Also, our benefactor, the leader of the Tuvalu Marine, Captain Iefata Paeniu was there to see the delegation off.

This type of island visits that the Prime Minister now was going on, takes place every four years; just before an election and just after. This was the newly elected Prime Minister's first visit. He would repeat such a visit before the next election, at the end of his period in office. The Prime Minister visited usually three islands at a time until he had visited all nine.

The weather forecasts were not good but the Prime Minister decided: "The trip is on." His wife was just as brave and optimistic as he.

The Prime Minister spoke to us on board and listened closely to the story of the Seladon's dramatic shipwreck. He requested an English version of Lars Oftedal's book about the Seladon that we showed him.

The crew waiting for the Prime Minister's arrival at the port.

The journey started in the afternoon, and we sailed south all night. The length of the journey was 300 km. At dawn, the ship was in position outside Niulakita. We woke to a beautiful sight, a small picturesque Pacific island with green coconut palms that towered high into the air all over the entire island. We could make out the houses where people lived, in the clearings among the trees, near the beach. The launch that was to take us in to the island was prepared and lowered along the side of the ship. The shuttle through the reef was a considerable strain on the boats. During our last trip to the islands to the north, one of the launches had been damaged, so now the ship had only the one boat on board as well as several rubber dinghies. The launch was rigged with chairs and equipped at the bow with the country's flag. After a solemn boarding of the delegation, they headed for the foaming surf.

The Prime Minister and his wife have taken place in the launch that is to set them ashore on the island.

The first group arrived safely ashore and were accompanied to the school for breakfast. On the menu were black birds, the same kind of birds that the Norwegian sailors ate over 100 years ago. It turned out that this was black terns; we thought that they did not look like small "black crows" as the Seladon crew had called them.

The launch returned and was soon back at the ship. The next transfer was us and three women with a little baggage. Our landing was not as successful. There was a sudden stop when we hit a concrete ramp on the beach that resulted in most of us fell over.

When I walked up the steep, sandy beach, I tried to imagine how the Norwegians in the same place 112 years ago had struggled up on dry land towards the cottages.

Wincent Rege on Niulakitas beach

Most of the 35 inhabitants were of course occupied with the Prime Minister's visit. We were greeted by a nice young man. He was well dressed, with a freshly ironed dark "lava lava" and a white shirt. It turned out that he was the meteorologist on the island. After we had explained to him why we were visiting the island, he pointed out the direction of the old cemetery. He promised to come and help us later, after his duties were done.

Very soon we ourselves found the tombstone for Tollak Olsen Vestbo. We weeded out some large leaves and took pictures. Gjert Meling had a thrilling search when he in 1996 had been helped by the islanders to clear brush and trees that had overgrown the old cemetery on the island.

The old cemetery on the island.

A man, who helped Meling at that time, told us that they finally had found the stone lying with the lettering facing down. That indicated that in the course of a hundred years it had slipped forward from the vertical position and finally tipped over. Now it was supported from behind, and was slightly tilted backwards. In this way it will remain stable, but the herbs with their large leaves will continue to grow in height with the top of the gravestone.

It amazed us how deep the letters were carved into the stone. It almost looked as if it had been carved yesterday. The many years it had laid overturned with the lettering down, served surely as protection against wear and tear on the stone. Around the grave were placed a number of smaller stones in a rectangular pattern. This was something we had noticed at other burial sites we had visited on some of the other islands.

The text on the tombstone was:

TOLLAK OLSEN
STAVANGER NORGE
DØD 14.9.1896

In Tuvalu, it is natural to just use the first name of people. That we learned from the female teacher on the island. We hesitated a bit when she asked if we had visited the grave of Tollak, it sounded almost as if she had known him personally. Many were interested in looking at the picture we had of Tollak, some came and asked to see it repeatedly. A young man said: "This is also our history." Some say that it was Abraham Hallvardson Tjelta that carved the letters and shaped the tombstone for Tollak, but this is uncertain, as it is not stated in the crew's recorded testimony. But the stone was impressively beautiful. I don't understand how they could have found such a hard, flat, and sculpted stone on this coral island. We never saw one like it on any of the islands we visited.

After the visit to Tollak's grave, we went on a walk around the island on our own. We studied the shape of the land, the reef and the beach. We found the open pit mine where the guano was dug out. There were now pools where the guano mass had previously been. With sandals we waded in the pools. We could easily see the bottom of the pools in the clear water, but the rough stone-like residue from the open pit mine and the sharp corals could easily cut our feet.

The Meteorologist and his friend changed after a while to every day clothes, and we joined them in crab hunting in between the coconut palms. The small crabs hid under plant residues near the palm trees. Neither these crabs, nor some larger coconut crabs that we saw on Nukulaelae are mentioned in the reports from the Seladon crew.

We were shown all the ponds on the island, including some deeper ponds, where the women 100 years ago swam and caught eels with their nets and where the Norwegians had as many as 20 turtles trapped. Still there were eels in the ponds.

The ponds are partially connected to each other. Since there were openings in the bottom of the ponds down through the coral, the water was connected to the ocean and the water level controlled by the tides. We became very excited when they asked us if we wanted to see a turtle nest to the north on the island. Right at the edge of the horizontal island surface, just before the terrain began to slant down into the water, had a turtle made a nest and covered it with sand.

Around the turtle nest there was a wire fence. The purpose of keeping the turtles fenced is that they want to feed them until they grow really big and thus improve their chances of survival in the wild.

Quantities of the black birds that the Seladon crew subsisted on flew over this particular grove of trees on the island. The birds are barely visible above the trees.

Ragnar Hellesto by the pond where eels were caught and where the crew from the Seladon kept turtles in captivity.

The remains of guano mining.

Our two helpers that showed us around Niulakita Island. Meteorologist in yellow T-shirt.

Later in the day we were invited to lunch with the Prime Minister and his party in the Maneapa, the community centre. The building was used both for parties and political meetings. The walls of the building were only a half meter high. Over the walls it was open to the outside all the way up to the roof that rested on pillars. In this way the building was fully ventilated.

There were rules about how to move about in there. People should not walk across the floor, but go along the walls. If there were mats on the floor, we must not step on them; these were for people to sit on. All were assigned seats on the floor. We exerted ourselves to sit correctly, with heels facing each other, because the soles of our feet should never point at others. Our shoes were placed outside.

Plates were handed out, they were made of woven palm leaves, and we could help ourselves from a table with the most delectable dishes; meat, fish, chicken, vegetables and rice.

Cutlery was not used; we all ate with our fingers and drinks we got from our respective coconut equipped with a suitable hole. In this way there were no waste that could contaminate or spoil the beautiful island, everything that was used was organic, and went back to nature. The hall was decorated with large bunches of bananas in the big window openings.

The Prime Minister gave a lively speech in their language. We understood as much as that he promised them funds to improve telecommunications, for which the meteorologists had submitted a written request. The manuscript for the speech was in the hand of the secretary sitting on the floor. The Prime Minister now and then glanced at him and he got the cue that he needed to continue the speech.

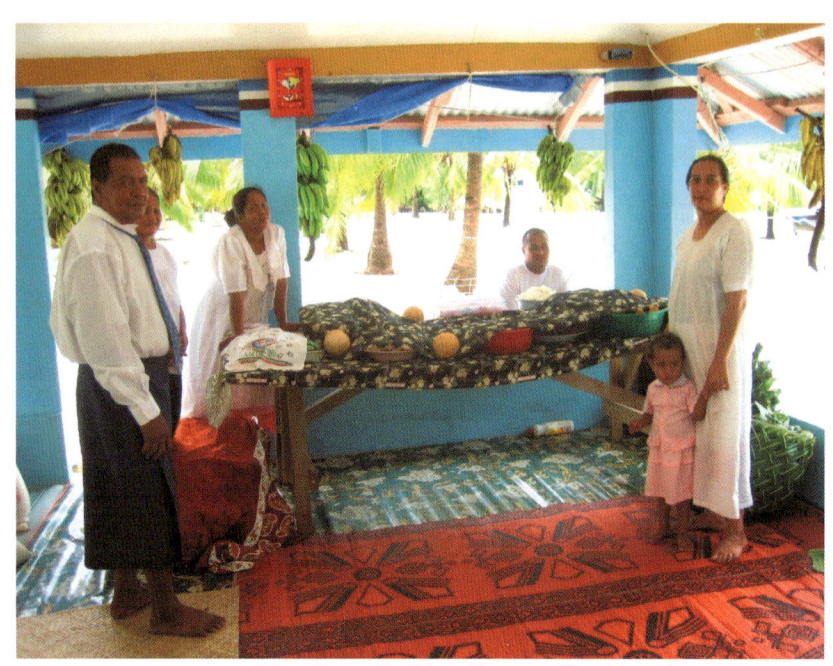

The lunch table is ready.

The Prime Minister gives his speech.

Ragnar Hellesto eats lunch on Niulakita.
The Prime Minister's wife is sitting in the background.

On the island there were in total 35 inhabitants. Inside the hall, we were probably about 20 people, while some stood outside and listened. The entertainment consisted of singing, alternately from the hosts and every other time from the delegation. We perceived the songs as gospel-like. This went on for about an hour. At the end, the guests were presented with gifts of beautiful hand-made fans of bast.

Suddenly we noticed that the strength of the wind increased and the tops of the palm trees began to sway. It is the ship's and the boat crews that determines when the return trip should start. They keep an eye on the height of the waves and they can quickly increase. Soon sounded the signal that warned about returning to the ship.

Beforehand, we had been told that it was our group that was in the first launch back to the ship. Just when the signal sounded, I was out in the village taking pictures. Since I did not want to be the one delaying the return trip, I ran immediately back to the beach. Thus I did not get the opportunity to take proper farewell and thank everyone for their hospitality as I had wanted. We will try to send down this book in English, and in this way thank the residents for the great experience we had on their island.

A nice picture of some of the children on Niulakita.

It was sad to leave Niulakita and see it get smaller and smaller as we went to the northeast. Again my thoughts went back to the men of the Seladon that for so many years ago had sailed towards the island in the opposite direction. This was the amazing sight that met the Norwegian sailors as they approached the island.

It was a beautiful little island.

Departing from Niulakita.
The opening in the reef can be seen in the background.

Soon we were on our way towards the next island, Nukulaelae, the island where the Prime Minister was born. New surprises were waiting.

We slept too well on 2nd class in the bottom of the boat, and there was no porthole to look out of. When we came up on deck in the morning, the ship was anchored, and the delegation had already gone by boat to the island. The explanation for the early disembarkation was that the tide was going towards low-tide, so in order to reach land the delegation had to leave at the crack of dawn. In order for us to get ashore, they had to drop us a ½ km from the island. From there we could wade ashore on a coral plateau. With water to over the knees, we waded toward the shore and ended up on the beach.

We landed on the outskirts of the village and asked for the place where the delegation had gone ashore. To our surprise, we suddenly heard someone speaking to us in Norwegian. It was the friendly Sonia Toematagi Dahl who had got wind that a couple of tourists were with the delegation on their trip. Sonia was 18 years old and has a Norwegian father.

She made sure we were able to participate in most activities and taught us much about Nukulaelae and the island life. Soon we were all aboard a small boat. The trip went over a several kilometer wide lagoon to another long stretched island that was partly owned by Sonia's grandfather (mother's father). Here they had a picnic for the delegation and representatives from Nukulaelae. We got to see and taste the coconut crab, which has some very large and strong claws that allow them to open coconuts.

Again we could leave after a meal for which no plastic bags would be filled with plastic cutlery and waste.

Healthy food served from a Tuvaluan lunch table
made from palm leaves.

Ragnar Hellesto with two fine specimens
of the coconut crab.

A woman prepares black terns. The same birds that nourished the Seladon crew on Niulakita.

Roasted Tuvaluan pig annum 2008.
1897:"When there was a party for the family, a birthday or alike they always roasted a whole pig. They roasted the whole pig on a stone, and had a very solemn and happy time together."

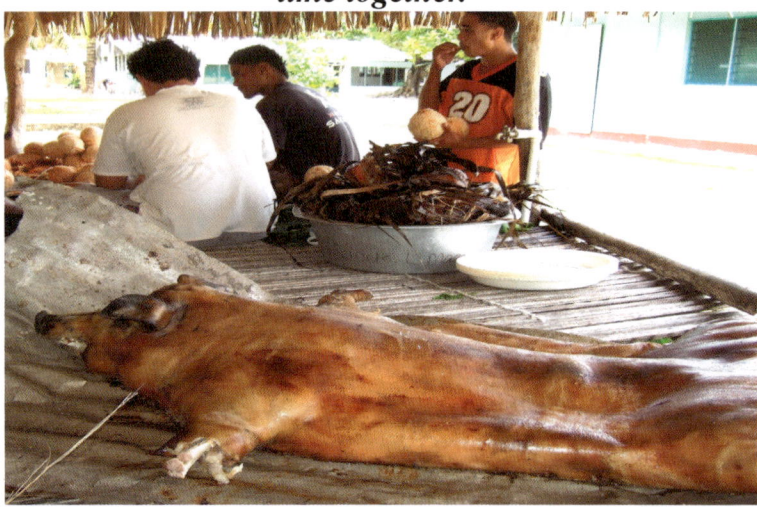

The Seladon crew drained coconut tree sap in 1896. It is still done the same way today.

A very nice young man steered one of the boats we used to cross the lagoon. He had been exiled from his own island for a period of time because of his youthful energy and desire for excitement. He had climbed up and moved about on the roof of the largest church in Funafuti. But he was fully integrated with all the other young people on Nukulaelae and enjoyed his work. I am sure that his life was enriched by the stay on the island, where he for a time was exiled.

Whenever human relations problems occurred in these small communities, they had to be settled immediately. This was done by forcing those involved to sit down and talk to each other, often with many people present.

The meeting in the great Maneapa with a speech of the Prime Minister was done in the same way as on Niulakita, but since the population was several hundred here, we were probably over a hundred people in the hall. Again our shoes were placed outside. We all sat on mats on the floor, the politicians also. We were assigned our place next to the back exit, but eventually we moved around to film and take pictures.

In addition to the song, both men and women performed several Polynesian dances that I filmed with my camera. The women had to leave their work in the kitchen, put on a grass skirt and perform the dance. Also the men who danced afterwards had grass skirts. They were also wearing decorations of green palm leaves around their neck and on their head. They all danced barefoot.

Traditional Tuvaluan dance.

Norwegian Sonia that was so fond of dancing, and had participated in dance competitions abroad, had to unfortunately do kitchen duties while the dancing was going on. She had spent so much time with us instead of on the kitchen tasks she was assigned.

She introduced us to her uncles, aunts and her grandfather Toematagi Samuelu. He was a former governor and magistrate who in 1982 had been awarded the empire medal by Britain's Queen Elizabeth II.

Sonia's parents, Terje and Emma Dahl currently live in Australia. Terje has written several books and runs among other things, the Internet magazine www.sydhav.no.

Sonia Toematagi Dahl with her
grandfather Toematagi Samuelu.

Nukulaelae was a very beautiful island with its large lagoon and the long stretch of small islands located in a circle around the lagoon. Upon departure this time we had more time to say goodbye and we experienced the warmth that these islanders are able to express.

It got dark way too soon. When everyone that came with the ship was well on board, it was so dark that we no longer could see Nukulaelae. Nevertheless an attempt was made in the dark to transport a pig and some materials to the island with the use of the launch. Even with the help of a powerful light from the ship and good flashlights the crew could not find the opening in the reef, and had to return to the ship. The lucky pig had to be hoisted on board again and thereby got its life extended on Funafuti ...

When we woke up the next day, the ship was docked at Funafuti.

Once again there was no one on the ship when we came up on deck. This time it was not because we had overslept. The reason for their absence was that the delegation and the crew preferred to sleep at home in their own beds and thus left the ship once it had docked at night.

Filled with impressions the time had come to leave Tuvalu. At the airport our Tuvaluan friends met up and put pearl necklaces around our necks and waved goodbye. A fire truck drove to the end of the runway with full sirens to clear it for children and ball-playing youngsters. Moped riders that were about to bring food to the pig pens on the opposite side of the runway had to hurry. Soon we would be able to observe the distinctive Funafuti atoll from the air.

As the plane climbed toward the non-existing clouds, I thought I could make out some figures waving farewell from the Prime Ministers courtyard at the end of the airstrip ...

***

A bit about Niulakita

Niulakita is the southernmost of the nine islands of Tuvalu. It lies a days sailing south of the main island Funafuti. The island is about 1 kilometer long and ½ kilometer wide. It is a coral island, but not a classic atoll like many others that have a lagoon at the centre. The size of the ponds located in the middle of the island is partly a result of the open pit mining where guano was previously extracted. The cross profiles of the island shows a lower terrain where the ponds are located. This must have been a favourite place for birds for thousands of years.

The island is located 10 ° 45 'South, 179 ° 30' East in the Pacific Ocean.

Niulakita is the island of Tuvalu that has the best agricultural land, therefore it is relatively self-sufficient. The ships that sail between the islands often only puts out a small rubber raft on the water and delivers the mail to the residents and then departs immediately.

In 2008, our plan was to follow such a supply ship to Niulakita. If the plan had succeeded, we probably would not have had many minutes on the island. We were really lucky, I must say, that we were able to travel with the Prime Minister's delegation and thus spend several hours there.

It is possible to apply for permission to go with a supply ship to the island and then remain there until the next ship comes. This was something that we already had considered as a plan B, but the stay on the island would have been long, perhaps a month or more. In our baggage we had equipped ourselves with both canned food and tents so that if we were in for a longer stay, we would be as self sufficient as possible.

The meteorologist that we had many conversations with told us that he liked the life on Niulakita so well, that he would apply to extend his stay. His wife also worked there as a nurse. The meteorologist's work was to take measurements of the climate and precipitation at the weather station on the island and make reports to the authorities.

The island also had a priest and a teacher. The island school was started in 1980. Today coconuts and copra are no longer exported from the island as in the old days, perhaps only a few bags are sent to relatives living on other islands. Many of the houses and buildings that we saw on the island had recently been built. The reason being that a storm a few years ago had done great damage to the island.

I'll include a little information about the island that I read in a booklet that was published by FAO, one of the organizations of the UN. It is an agronomic study of Niulakitas resources and also some history. I read it at the university library on Fiji in 2007 and later at the library on Funafuti in 2008. I took some notes from this booklet that is the source of some of the factual information about Niulakita which here follows:

The island was discovered by Alvaro Mendena in 1595. He gave the island the name La Solitaria which means the lonely.

The whaler Georg Barnett from Nantucket gave it the name Rocky Island when he came across it in 1821. It was then uninhabited. Only a single coconut palm towered into the air amid all the shrubs. Later, the island had the names Niurakita and Sophia Island.

A judicial commissioner named Le Hunt from the British Admiralty found in 1883 two families living on the island. A family from Samoa and one from Vaitupu. In total they were ten people. One or two acres was planted with young coconut palms and some Pandanus trees. Since 1880, smaller working groups from Vaitupu lived there and ran the plantation with coconut palms.

The German company "Company Ruge & Co." bought Niulakita in 1884 from Vaitupu for 400 Chilean dollars.

The American businessman Harry Jay Moors bought the island towards the end of the 1800s. He lived on Samoa. He started the extraction of guano and the production of copra from coconuts. As mentioned earlier it was Moors that owned the island when the crew from the Seladon was there.

He later claimed payment for their stay. Lars Oftedal wrote a sarcastic article in Stavanger Aftenblad in 1897 about the American's claim:

The American Moors. You remember his name, the Samoa man that owns the Sofia Island, which incidentally is under control by the British government. He must be a smart guy this American. Oh yes, they all are. But imagine this one sent a bill for these shipwrecked people for their stay on the island to the consulate in Sydney asking for the sum of 165,184 pounds. In Norway it would be about 3000 kroner. These are the boys that know how, these Americans. Because they helped to clear the island, collected some turtles from the sea and ate some coconuts. 3000 kroner for that! Oh yes, the carpenter is buried there. He probably wants money for that too. About 200 kroner for each man, because they were able to crawl up on the beach and save their lives until some people came and rescued them ... three Thousand!

Harry J. Moors sold the island in 1914 to EFH Allan of the Samoa Shipping and Trading Company. Samoan merchants continued production of copra until 1926.

In the year 1926, the island was purchased by the firm Philip Burn & Company of Sydney. They owned it until 1944 when it was sold to the Western Pacific High Commission, which meant that it was purchased by the United Kingdom.

In 1944, the island had for a period of time been uninhabited. The British found the island overrun by rats and 30 cattle in good shape.

One of the Brits that spent the night there during the visit to the island woke suddenly as he was knocked out of bed.

Above him stood an ox. It was thirsty and wanted to drink the water out of the four buckets that the bed legs had been placed in. The buckets of water were there to prevent the rats from crawling into the bed.

Late in the 1940s a land commissioner named Lake travelled around on the different islands of Tuvalu. He proposed to give the island to Niutao that was overcrowded, so they could move people over to Niulakita. In 1949 arrived the first group from Niuato to stay on the island and the production of copra started up again. Niutao lies second furthest north of the nine islands of Tuvalu. To this very day it is still the Niutao Island Council which is responsible for maintaining a suitably large population on Niulakita.

It is very popular to live on Niulakita, which makes it necessary for people on Niutao to apply for permission to live there three years at a time. For tourists who want to spend the night on Niulakita, they must apply for permission from Secretary Niutao. If someone comes by a private boat, it must be cleared in Funafuti, both before and after the visit.

The table below shows the historical census records made on Niulakita over the years:

Year 1911 - 4 people
Year 1931 - 40 people
Year 1947 - 21 people
Year 1963 - 42 people
Year 1968 - 54 people
Year 1973 - 65 people
Year 1979 - 65 people
Year 1983 - 95 people
Year 2008 - 35 people

Above: Recently built houses among palm trees on Niulakita.

The church on Niulakita.

A bit about Tuvalu

Tuvalu is an island nation in the Pacific Ocean, located between Australia and Hawaii. It consists of nine coral islands. Five of them are classic atolls with a large lagoon in the middle and small elongated islands around. The other four consist of a single island, where some have a small lagoon in the middle of the island. The distance between each islands is about a day's sailing. On the map one can see that the islands are located along a long curved line from the north to the south-east.

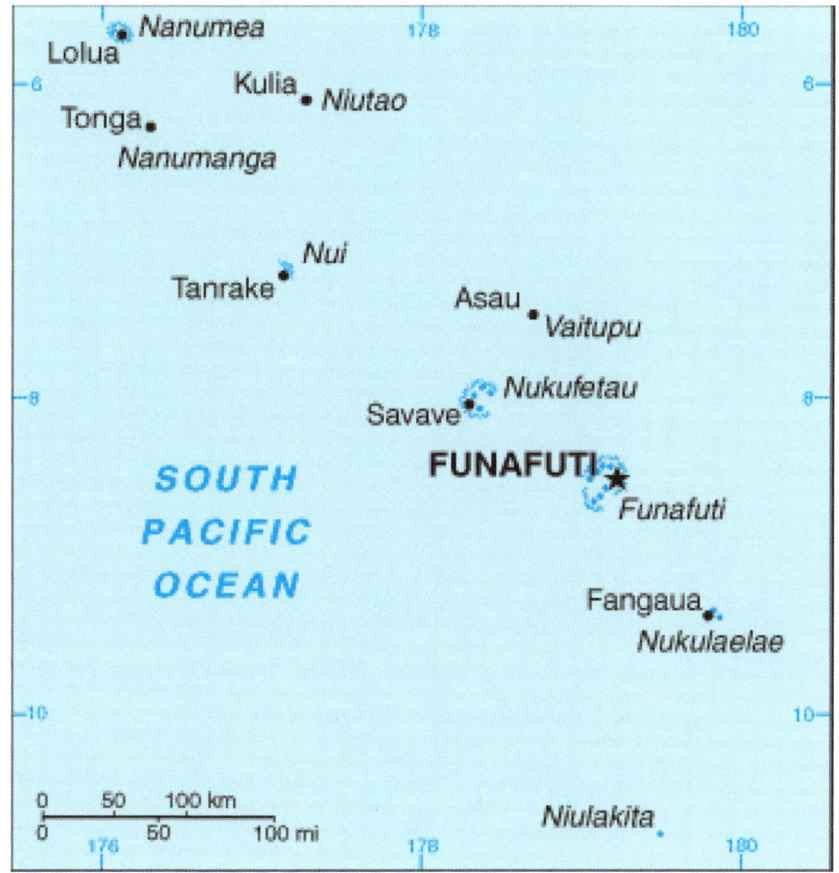

The people of Tuvalu are known to be among the friendliest in the world. The country has only 10,000 inhabitants spread over the nine islands. Almost half of the population live on the main island of Funafuti. The main island is an atoll consisting of many smaller islands that form a circle around a lagoon. The largest island is called Fongafale. There is where the airstrip and the town hall are placed.

A picture I took from the plane on the way home from Tuvalu in 2008. Shows Fongafale, Funafuti.

Peruvian slave traders called black-birders, combed the Pacific in the period 1862-1864. Many people were taken prisoner. 171 people from Funafuti and 250 people from Nukulaelae were lured aboard slave ships and never returned. That was perhaps the reason why the residents of Niulakita in 1896 at first were very frightened when the lifeboat with the crew from the Seladon came to the island. The men armed themselves with knives and axes, while the women fled into the woods. When the Norwegians came ashore, they were immediately asked if everyone in the lifeboat were white men. Only then, when they were reassured did they continue to help the shipwrecked sailors.

Tuvalu was called Ellis Island until 1975 when it was separated from the Gilbert Islands, a group of islands which lies further north. In 1978, Tuvalu received their independence. Then the country became a constitutional monarchy within the Commonwealth of Nations with Queen Elizabeth II as head of state. She is represented there by a Governor-General.

The local parliament has 15 members, where each island is represented. Its members choose a prime minister as head of government. Elections are held every four years. At the local level, informal authority is also held by some older and respected people.

From nature's side, the country is not very fruitful. There is almost no drinking water and the soil is poorly suited for food production. Since there are almost no natural resources on the islands, the main source of income is fishing, as well as some mining and tourism. Some of the men on the islands are seamen working on foreign ships, among others German ships.

Revenue sources for the government is foreign assistance and sale of fishing licenses, as the country owns large ocean areas. The country has also managed to put aside revenues that successfully have been invested in equity funds. Thus, the country can now use the returns from these as a source of income. A bit like our own oil fund in Norway.

Another special revenue source for Tuvalu is the sale of internet domains. A Tuvaluan Internet address ends with the letters TV. This letter combination is so interesting for many commercial firms that they want to use it for their websites. There is money in this, in fact over 5 million dollar since 1999.

The islands are very low and are thus threatened by any future rise of the sea level. If sea levels should begin to rise the population can be forced to evacuate the country. We sincerely hope that the idyllic islands does not disappear under water, but continue to remain as at present.

The Tall Ships Races in Stavanger

The harbour in Stavanger during The Tall Ships Races 2011.
Photo: Tor Andreas Tonnesen.

From 28 July to 31 July 2011 Stavanger hosted the The Tall Ships Races, which is an international sailing regatta for large sailing ships. The races are intended to encourage international friendship and sailing training for young people. The races are arranged annually between various cities in Europe. To allow a ship to participate, the age of at least half of the crew must be under 25 years.

The first time the race was held was in 1956, when 20 of the last remaining big sailing ships took part in a race that went from England to Portugal. The Norwegian ship "Christian Radich" came then in 2nd in the competition. The one that came up with the idea for the races was the English solicitor Bernard Morgan. He convinced several other eminent Englishmen to join him in arranging the races. The regatta was organized to mark the final end of the era of sailing ships, and to build good friendships and understanding among young people from different countries.

In Stavanger there arrived 70 beautiful sail ships the July days in 2011. The event was a great success. The organizers estimated that there were approximately 450 000 people along the docks around the bay and out on the fjord to see the ships and experience the atmosphere of the city.

For us the tall ship festival was a good opportunity to talk to people about the Seladon shipwreck and do a little promotion of the book. We had put on T-shirts with a picture of the Seladon in front, in addition to some flyers in both Norwegian and English that we handed out to people that we came to talk to.

These days in July during the Tall Ships Races in Stavanger were our little summer vacation. Every day we went into Stavanger to visit. We walked along the docks, admired the ships and went aboard most of them. People we talked to on board the foreign ships was handed a flyer about the Seladon shipwreck in English. When the ships sailed out to the next port of call, there were many on board that now had heard a little about Stavanger's own Robinson Crusoe story.

We also met some descendants of the Seladon crew during these summer days in Stavanger. On board the ketch "Svanhild" we got to know Reidar Tjelta Knapstad from Floro. He was the grandson of Abraham Hallvardson Tjelta. It was fascinating to learn that the "Svanhild" like the Seladon was built at the end of the 1800s. He had previously sailed around the world with the same vessel. His wife and daughter came along with him to the Tall Ships Races and served as crew members.

Reidar Tjelta Knapstad aboard the sailing ship Svanhild.
Reidar is the grandchild of Abraham Tjelta,
who was a seaman on the Seladon.
Photo: Tor Andreas Tonnesen.

On Sunday we went to Tungenes lighthouse to see the ships off. Here we met a man that was the great grandson of one of the sailors on the Seladon. He told us that several members of his family had been named after his great grandfather, the sailor Marcelius Aske. We got the idea that perhaps a meeting could be arranged for the descendants of the Seladon crew at the next Tall Ships Races in Stavanger.

From Stavanger the sailing ships went on to Halmstad in Sweden. On board there were about 200 young people from the district that got the opportunity to come along on the ships as trainees. But it's not just young people who have the opportunity to join the race. On the home page of Sail Training International they report that several people of both 70 and 80 years of age, has sailed along as trainees and enjoyed the experience of working with others against the temperamental and unpredictable sea. So if you like the idea of experiencing a journey from a bygone era, to hear the creaking from the rig and see the great square sails flutter in the wind, why not apply as a trainee and experience what it is to travel by sail.

Epilogue

In connection with our work on the book, it has been very enjoyable to meet some of the descendants of the Seladon crew.

Captain Adolph Emil Jaeger had three brothers and a sister. His sister Olufine Katrin Jaeger was married to Captain Helmik Gabriel Eriksen. The great grandchild of the captain's sister, Anne- Lise Bjornsen, was of great help during the work on the book and gave us much useful information, and a wonderful photo of Captain Jaeger.

We wanted to find out what had happened with Lars Marthinius Tonnesen who had written such personal letters home to his family. One summer day in August 2011 we traveled expectantly to Hundvåg in Stavanger. There we were to meet the daughter of Trygve Tonnesen named Helen Ekornrod and the daughter of Tonnes Tonnesen named Martha Okland. The grandchildren of the steward on the Seladon were very enthusiastic and had a lot of knowledge about all aspects of the Seladon shipwreck.

We spent a very pleasant day at home with them. We saw a piece of paper where Lars had written a short resume of the story and a copy of the first edition of Oftedals book from 1897 that they had kept.

Helen Ekornrod told us that she would have loved to come with us to Niulakita.

We were told a little story during our visit:

Lars's wife must have been very excited about the return of her husband after months of grief, loss and longing. Inger Elisabeth Tonnesen had in 1897 brought along the children Margit and Trygve and started the long trip from the Kalhammaren, down to the centre of Stavanger and out to Skansekaien on Holmen. It was a dark and cold October evening. No street lights. Perhaps morning would come before the steamship Venus arrived. When Inger Elisabeth and the children had come down to the main road towards the city, she had changed her mind and gone back to the farm again.

Helen Ekornrod and Martha Okland.
Grandchildren of Lars M.Tonnesen.

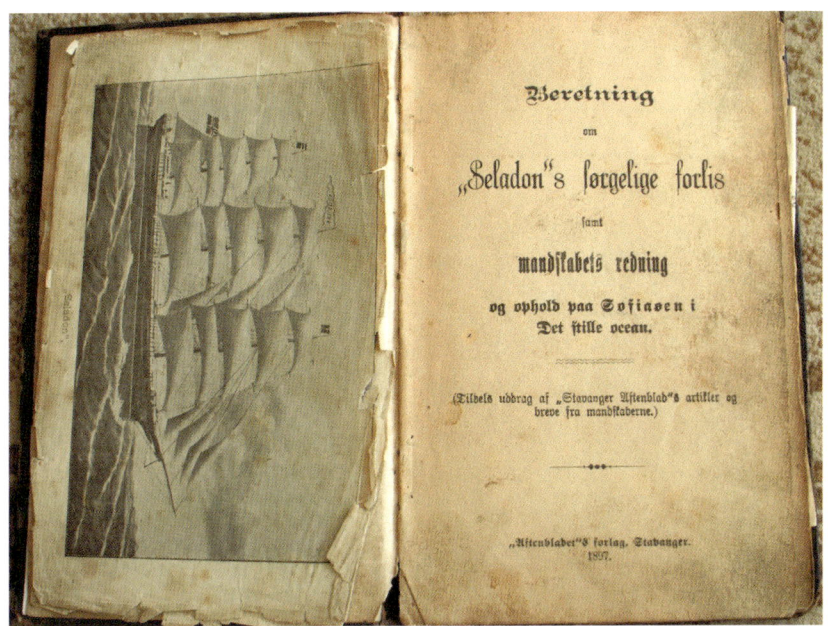

The first edition of the book by Lars Oftedal from 1897 and a piece of paper where Lars M. Tonnesen wrote down a summary of the story has been kept by the descendants.

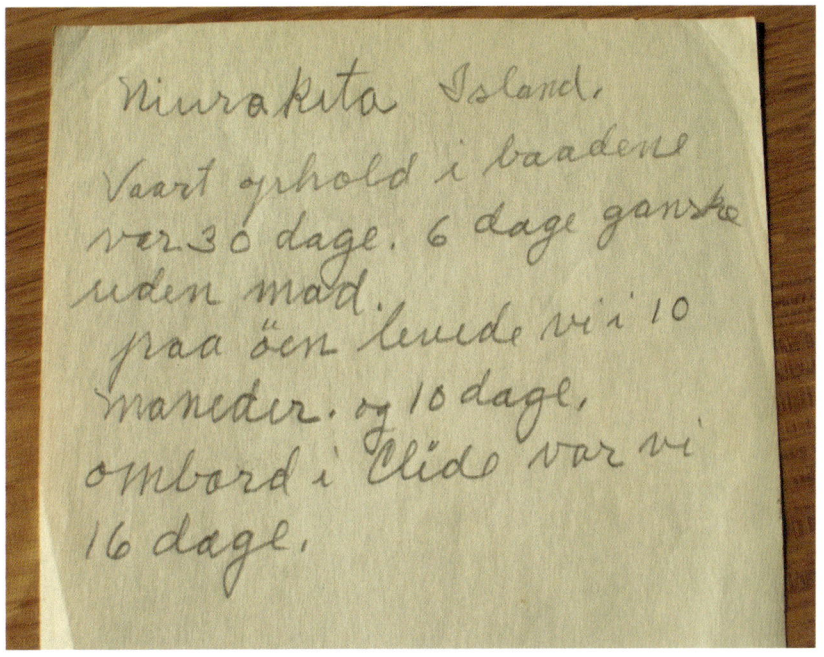

In Randaberg, we visited Ragnhild Bo who is the granddaughter of Tollak Olsen Vestbo. The lusty lady, who had managed to become 93 years old, was so healthy and vibrant that we that have reached the 60s got an a-ha experience about getting older. It was as if we got a supply of positive energy from the the nice lady and left there in a cheerful mood. Ragnhild had also heard Abraham Tjelta give the talk about the Seladon's shipwreck at an event in Sola. She was only 15 years old at the time, and had not dared to tell Abraham who she was.

Ragnhild Bo, grandchild of Tollak Olsen Vestbo.

We hope you enjoyed our book.

Should any of the readers or other descendants of the crew
like to meet us or have a chat, we would be delighted.

Please contact us by phone or e-mail:
wincentrege@yahoo.no

This book will be available at:

www.amazon.com

www.createspace.com/3781605

Various museums in Stavanger.

***

Thank you

Thanks to the staff at Stavanger Aftenblad for their great service; Tarald Aano, Kjell Arvid Berge, Hege Solbakken Sabo og Reidun Wold.

Thanks to Ragnar Hellesto for our pleasant trip to Tuvalu and Niulakita in 2008.

Thanks to Svein Terje Vestbo for the received material and that you shared your knowledge of the Seladon shipwreck with us. Svein Terje is from Vikebygd in Ryfylke. He is great grandchild of Tollak Olsen Vestbo.

Thanks to Martha Okland and Helen Ekornrod for friendly visits and the use of private family photos.

Thanks to Ragnhild Bo for friendly visits and the use of private family photos.

Thanks to Anne-Lise (Lisen) Bjornsen for private pictures of Captain Adolph Emil Jaeger and useful information, including the hints on the Imsland drawings and Seladon's song.

Thanks to Gro Stromnes Dybedal for letting us use the Henry Imsland drawings. Henry Imsland was for many years Stavanger Aftenblad's artist. Gro is the granddaughter of Henry Imsland.

Thanks to Gjert Meling and Halvor Pedersen for the inspiration and for the nice visit and chat about the Seladon when we returned from Niulakita in 2008.

Thanks to Tor Andreas Tonnesen from Flekkefjord for the photos from the The Tall Ships Races.

Thanks to Anna Tjelta for private photograph of Abraham Hallvardson Tjelta.

Thanks to Sola Photo\ Elin Flaate.

Thanks to everyone who helped us at the State Archive in Stavanger.

Thanks to everyone who helped us at the City Archive in Stavanger.

Thanks to everyone who helped us at the Stavanger Maritime Museum.

Thanks to everyone who helped us on Tuvalu.

Thanks to everyone interested in sailing that we talked to during The Tall Ships Races in Stavanger.

Thanks to Magne Vilfred Hansen for translating our book to English.

Sources and Literature:

The "Seladon". An account of the accident and the crew's stay on the Sofia Island."
First published in 1897 by Lars Oftedal / Stavanger Aftenbladet.

Interview with Ingebret Hognestad in Stavanger Aftenblad January 12th 1935.

«Vindetreet. Sogeskrift for Vindafjord 1996»
Article written by Svein Terje Vestbo.

"Seladon and her men."
Novel by Halvor Pedersen from 1981.

"The story of Lars Oftedal."
Biography of Berge Furre from 1990.

www.wikipedia.org

www.sydhav.no

www.vulkaner.no

www..sailtraininginternational.org

www.janeresture.com

About the authors

Wincent Rege born in 1949. He is now retired. Has previously worked as a teacher, farmer, structural engineer and janitor. Travels around the world as a backpacker every winter to more new exciting places. The highlight was when he visited Tuvalu and the Seladon Island Niulakita in 2008.

Eli Rege born in 1951. She is a nurse and line dance instructor. Runs Sola Home Hostel with Wincent where foreign guests rent rooms in their house. She has a dream that the story about the Seladon in the future will be filmed.

Malvin Rege born in 1977 and works in the oil industry. The son of Wincent and Eli. Wrote on the book between baby care and changing nappies in the summer of 2011.

Wincent, Malvin, Daniel and Eli writing the book.

SELADONs forlis

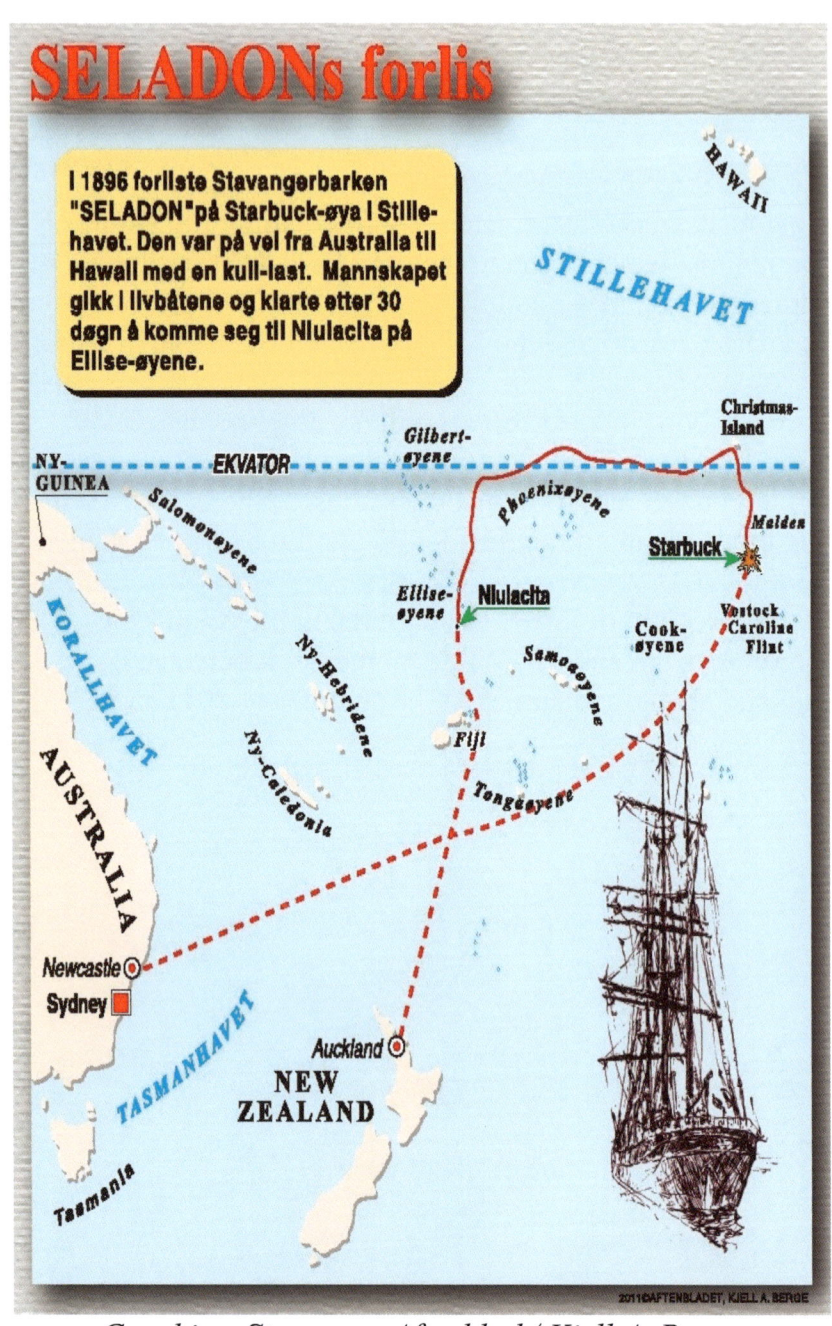

I 1896 forliste Stavangerbarken "SELADON" på Starbuck-øya I Stillehavet. Den var på vei fra Australia til Hawaii med en kull-last. Mannskapet gikk i livbåtene og klarte etter 30 døgn å komme seg til Niulacita på Ellise-øyene.

Graphics: Stavanger Aftenblad / Kjell A. Berge.

146

Printed in Great Britain
by Amazon

41753201R00087